About the Author

Lon Milo DuQuette is a preeminent scholar, magician, and speaker. The author of fourteen critically acclaimed books on magick and the occult, DuQuette is one of the most respected and entertaining writers and lecturers in the field of Western Magick. Visit him online at www.lonmiloduquette.ning.com.

To Write to the Author

If you wish to contact the author or would like more information about this book, please write to the author in care of Llewellyn Worldwide and we will forward your request. Both the author and publisher appreciate hearing from you and learning of your enjoyment of this book and how it has helped you. Llewellyn Worldwide cannot guarantee that every letter written to the author can be answered, but all will be forwarded. Please write to:

Lon Milo DuQuette
℅ Llewellyn Worldwide
2143 Wooddale Drive
Woodbury, MN 55125-2989
Please enclose a self-addressed stamped envelope for reply,
or $1.00 to cover costs. If outside the U.S.A., enclose
an international postal reply coupon.

Many of Llewellyn's authors have websites with additional information and resources. For more information, please visit our website at:

www.llewellyn.com

LOW MAGICK

IT'S ALL IN YOUR HEAD . . .
YOU JUST HAVE NO IDEA
HOW BIG YOUR HEAD IS

LON MILO DUQUETTE

Llewellyn Publications
Woodbury, Minnesota

FIRST EDITION
Tenth Printing, 2020

Cover design by Kevin R. Brown
Cover images: background © iStockphoto.com/Selahattin Bayram;
     brain © iStockphoto.com/Todd Harrison
Interior illustrations by Llewellyn art department, except: Pentagram of Solomon and
     Hexagram of Solomon on page 163 by Jacqueline A. Williams; Ganesha on pages
     118, 122–123, 126, and 129–131 by Wen Hsu

Llewellyn is a registered trademark of Llewellyn Worldwide Ltd.

Library of Congress Cataloging-in-Publication Data
DuQuette, Lon Milo, 1948–
  Low magick: it's all in your head, you just have no idea how big your
head is / Lon Milo DuQuette.—1st ed.
       p. cm.
  Includes bibliographical references (p.   ) and index.
  ISBN 978-0-7387-1924-5
  1. Magic. 2. DuQuette, Lon Milo, 1948– I. Title.
  BF1611.D8697 2010
  133.4'3—dc22
                          2010033880

Llewellyn Publications
A Division of Llewellyn Worldwide Ltd.
2143 Wooddale Drive
Woodbury, MN 55125-2989
www.llewellyn.com

Printed in the United States of America

*This little collection of memories, insights,
and embarrassments is lovingly dedicated to the members
of our Monday Night Magick Class past, present, and future.*

"There is no truth, only stories."

ZUNI SAYING

CONTENTS

ACKNOWLEDGEMENTS

The author wishes to recognize and thank the following individuals, whose encouragement and support over the years he shall always treasure: Constance Jean DuQuette, Jean-Paul DuQuette, Marc E. DuQuette, Judith Hawkins-Tillirson, Rick Potter, Donald Weiser, Betty Lundsted, Kat Sanborn, Patricia Baker, Chance Gardner, Vanese Mc Neil, David P. Wilson, Jonathan Taylor, Dr. Art Rosengarten, George Noory, Poke Runyon, James Wasserman, Rodney Orpheus, Robert Anton Wilson, Robert Larson, Brenda Knight, Sharon Sanders, Michael Miller, Michael Kerber, Jan Johnson, Brad Olsen, Janet Berres, Charles D. Harris, Michael Strader, Phyllis Seckler, Grady McMurtry, Israel Regardie, Helen Parsons Smith, Alan R. Miller, Ph.D., Clive Harper, William Breeze, John Bonner, Stephen King, and a very special thanks goes to Elysia Gallo and the wonderful team at Llewellyn Worldwide Ltd., for making this project such an enjoyable experience.

||||||||||||||||||||||||||||||||||||||||||||||||||||||||||||||||||||||||||||||||||||||||||||||||||||||||||||||||||||||||||||||

STORIES

I am always at a loss at how much to believe of my own stories.

WASHINGTON IRVING

Next to silence, stories are the most divine form of communication. Stories are alive. Stories are holy. Stories are gods that create universes and the creatures and characters that populate them. Stories bring to life all the triumphs and tragedies imagination and experience can summon to the mind. Stories speak directly to our souls.

Stories are magick.

As I begin the seventh decade of my life, I find myself more inclined to listen to a story than to study a text or reflect on an argument—more inclined to tell a story than to presume to teach a lesson or offer advice. Perhaps it is because as we grow older we have more stories to tell, and experience and wisdom conspire to add dimension, texture, and perspective to the lengthening register of our memories.

For whatever reason, I find myself at this season of my life unable to approach the subject of this book from any direction other than relating my personal experiences. This is not to say that I haven't integrated a great deal of theory and technical information within my nonchronological narratives. Indeed, I believe there is more than enough magical "how-to-ness" nestled within these pages to keep a motivated magician busy for some time. But it is the story that informs—the story that teaches—the story that reveals the magical "how-why-ness" (and in some instances, the "how-why not-ness") of the magician's life.

However, storytelling has certain disadvantages—foremost being the fact that memory is a fragile and subjective thing. Pain, regret, embarrassment, shame, wishful thinking, fantasy, and old-fashioned self-delusion constantly threaten the accuracy of our recollections of the past. Absolute objectivity is impossible. But unlike other mortals who lead less examined lives, the magician is obliged to keep a diary, and may refer to specific events recorded in his or her magical journals. I've relied heavily on my scribblings in the preparation of this book—a painfully embarrassing ordeal, I assure you.

Also, in the course of telling a magical story, one must consider the sensitivities and the privacy of other individuals, living or dead, who may be part of the action. Over the years I have been blessed to meet and work with some very wonderful and colorful characters, most of whom would not be recognizable personalities in our magical subculture, but a few of them I dare say might. So, I confess here and now that in certain places in this book I've changed names or made other literary adjustments to allow certain individuals to remain blissfully incognito.

I, of course, hope that you will enjoy this small collection of my memories, but I know that I can't possibly satisfy the taste and expectation of every reader. Perhaps this book will not be what you expected. Perhaps you will be disappointed that I haven't written yet another textbook or a more scholarly elucidation upon some great magical system or philosophical doctrine. If so, I hope you overlook my lack of apology, because I believe with this little book I am offering you something that can be far more powerful and enlightening—a gift of stories. I hope you accept them for what they are, and find your particular truth within them. For as the Zuni sages tell us, "There is no truth, only stories."

ZERO

|||||||||||||||||||||||||||||||||||||||||||||||||||||||||||||||||||||||||||||||||||||||||||||||||||||||||||||||||

FIRST LET'S TALK ABOUT FEAR

Speak of the Devil and he appears.

ITALIAN PROVERB

For a magician, it is better to be possessed by the demon than ignored by him.

RABBI LAMED BEN CLIFFORD

It is a sad fact (at least from my perspective) that not everyone who picks up this book and thumbs through it will end up buying it. It is also true that not everyone who buys it and takes it home will read it from cover to cover. So, just in case these opening remarks are the only words you will ever read from this book, I'm going to immediately exploit this fleeting moment we have together and impart to you in large uppercase letters the most important secret of magick—and of life:

DO NOT BE AFRAID!

Now! If you're short on time, please feel free to close the book and fearlessly get on with your life.

Do not get me wrong. It's good to be cautious. It's good to be wise. It's good to be measured and thoughtful in all your actions and behavior, but fear is poison to your magical practice and poison to your life. Please know that I am not preaching this gospel of fearlessness from the marble pulpit of righteousness and courage. On the contrary, I'm shouting it from the pasteboard megaphone of my own ignoble and cowardly character.

When I began my life as a practicing magician, it seemed like I was afraid of everything. When I rehearsed my first Pentagram and Hexagram rituals, I superstitiously monitored everything from my heartbeat to my horniness. I fantasized seeing things out of the corner of my eye, and recorded the most outlandish speculations in my diary.

I realize now that most of my fears of things that go bump in the night arose from the deepest stratum of my childhood religious programming. In less evasive words, I was still consciously and unconsciously brainwashed by my Christian upbringing—still trapped in a hostile universe that reverberated with the thundering curses of a wrathful God who frightens little children into acceptable behavior (so that they grow into obedient God-fearing *adult* little children). I was programmed by films and literature based upon that unwholesome doctrine of fear and self-loathing. Today, as I review my old diaries, it all seems pretty silly and melodramatic:

Performed Greater Invoking Pentagram Ritual of Fire for the first time. Later in the day broke a shoelace and had acid reflux.

or,

Slept with Mars talisman under my pillow—dreamed my father's corpse was eaten by seahorses—woke up with an erection.

I thank the gods that I had in those early years a knowledgeable, experienced, and competent magical mentor[1] who (when not projecting her own fears of low magick upon me)[2] mercilessly ridiculed my childish fears and helped me develop an attitude akin to that of a motivated research scientist who is driven by intense curiosity and a sense of scientific wonder. Remember Laura Dern's character in the film *Jurassic Park*, rolling up her sleeves and plunging her arm into a huge pile of dinosaur poop for a clue to the poor animal's tummy ache? Well, sometimes a magician is faced with even more disturbing psychological and spirit-world challenges, and the key to meeting those challenges is that same detached attitude of fearlessness, determination, and an unshakeable passion for enlightenment.

I recently received a letter from a magician who believed that her mood swings and other health issues were the result of her magical workings. Here's a portion of my letter back to her. I hope you find it encouraging.

Dear (name withheld),

Concerning mood swings and health issues *vis-à-vis* your magical practices, it's usually best to ascribe them to the normal demons of body chemistry and the stress of twenty-first century urban life. More often than not, a head cold or the flu isn't caused by backlash for a magical operation. Even if it were a negative reaction to your magical workings, your doubts and fears over the matter only serve to give the entities you fear permission and encouragement to keep feeding on your insecurities (and perhaps much more). By becoming preoccupied as to whether this pain

---

1 For my first few years of magical apprenticeship, I was privileged to study formally under Phyllis Seckler McMurtry (1917–2004), also known as Soror Meral, IX° OTO.

2 See chapter 1.

or that fever might be a demon messing with you, you voluntarily give the demon power to give you this pain or that fever—in a very real sense, the demon has evoked you!

Try to remain mindful that you'll probably live through all your magical workings (except perhaps the last one), and that nothing neutralizes the power of a pesky demon more than having its scariness ignored. Remember what it says in *Liber Librae:* "Humble thyself before thy Self, yet fear neither man not spirit. Fear is failure, and the forerunner of failure: and courage is the beginning of virtue."[3]

---

3 Aleister Crowley, *Liber Libræ Sub Figura XXX, The Book of the Balance* and *Magick, Liber ABA, Book Four.* Second revised edition, ed. Hymenaeus Beta (York Beach, ME: Weiser Books, Inc., 1997), 668. *Liber Libræ* itself was taken from a Golden Dawn paper, *On the General Guidance and Purification of the Soul.*

‖‖‖

ONE

THE DOGMA & RITUALS
OF LOW MAGICK

(Dogme et ritual de la bas magie)

Were the world understood.
Ye would see it was good.
A dance to a delicate measure.

ALEISTER CROWLEY[1]

I confess that the title of this chapter was intended to be a gentle poke at the great nineteenth-century esotericist, Eliphas Lévi, and his classic work, *The Dogma & Rituals of High Magic.*[2] Please don't assume that my irreverent little presumption is in any way an attempt

---

1 Aleister Crowley, *Collected Works, Orpheus. Vol. III* (Homewood, IL: Yogi Publications, 1978), 217.

2 Eliphas Lévi (1810–1875), pseudonym of Alphonse Louis Constant. *Dogme et ritual de la haute magie* was first published in 1854. Published most recently as *Transcendental Magic,* translated by A. E. Waite (York Beach, ME: Weiser Books, 2001).

on my part to compare my own work with Lévi's immortal text. Indeed, they are as different as day and night—or should I say *high* and *low*? (See how easily I have given myself a segue.)

I feel the necessity to establish here at the outset what I mean by the words "high magick" and "low magick." To be perfectly frank I've become very uncomfortable with both terms. They are each, in my opinion, universally misunderstood, misused, misapplied, misrepresented, and misinterpreted.

Some ceremonial magicians label their craft *high magick* to haughtily distinguish their art from the *low magick* of witchcraft. Conversely, some witches and Neopagans use the term sarcastically to brand ceremonial magicians and their ilk as snobs. Practical Qabalists, who presume their studies to be the only true high magick, use the terms to distance themselves from both ceremonial magicians and witches.

There are others who simply define low magick as being all things nature-based (outdoor magick), as opposed to ceremonial magick, à la the formal rituals of the Golden Dawn[3] or Aleister Crowley[4] (indoor magick). Here the terms *low* and *high* are diplomatically construed by both schools as being morally neutral; the two merely differing in character and application, and appealing to different spiritual personalities and tastes. Here, both the high and the low magician are relatively happy in their own worlds performing their own brand of magick.

There are many others, though, who define the highness and lowness of magick in ways that go way beyond discussing the differences between working in a lodge room temple or outside in a

---

3 Founded in 1888, the Order of the Golden Dawn was arguably the most influential magical society of the late nineteenth and early twentieth centuries. Aleister Crowley joined in 1898 and would soon become the catalyst in the events that would bring about the Order's destruction. The basic degree structure of the Golden Dawn would serve as the model for Crowley's own magical order, the A∴A∴

4 Ibid.

grove. For these people, "high magick" refers to a formal process of effecting change in one's environment by enlisting the aid of God and a heavenly hierarchy of *good* archangels, angels, intelligences, and spirits; and "low magick" refers to a formal process of effecting change by enlisting the aid of the devil (or devils), fallen angels, and infernal evil spirits and demons.

Obviously, in order to seriously consider the virtues of this perspective, a person must first be committed to a very particular (some might say "draconian") view of spiritual reality—one that is supported (or so the argument goes) by the scriptures and doctrines of the Christian, Moslem, or Jewish religions. For convenience sake, I will henceforth collectively (and respectfully) refer to these Bible-based religions by a term I coined just for conversations such as this. The word is:

"Chrislemew."[5]

One popular interpretation of these doctrines posits that humans are caught in the middle of a perpetual war between the armies of an absolutely *good* God in heaven above, and the minions of an absolutely *evil* devil in hell below. For reasons known only to God, the devil and his team have been placed in charge of human life on earth. Furthermore, according to this theory, God has especially charged the devil with the duty of tempting and tormenting human beings—perpetually prodding us to rebel against a curiously complex catalogue of commandments and divinely decreed roster of rules, irrational beliefs, and blindly obedient behavior that (if we follow the program faithfully) might[6] earn for us

---

5 See my book *Angels, Demons & Gods of the New Millennium* (York Beach, ME: Red Wheel/Weiser, 1997), 156.

6 Unfortunately, for the Christian born without "grace," right belief or good behavior in life will not be enough to save him or her from the dreadful flames of eternal hell. Sorry.

after death a ticket to eternal happiness in heaven with God and his good angels.

This parochial and highly polarized way of looking at things makes everything pretty simple. God is good. The devil is bad. Angels are good. Demons are bad. Heavenly stuff is high. Infernal stuff is low. For those who subscribe to the Chrislemew worldview, the choice of whether to pursue the path of high or low magick is a no-brainer. After all, who in their right mind would prefer to dabble with dangerous and deceitful evil demons from hell when instead one can safely seek the heavenly aid of the wholesome and well-behaved good angels of God Almighty?

From his high horse of spiritual piety, the high magician looks down upon low magicians who, in order to accomplish their nefarious ends, stand ready and willing to proffer their reprobate souls to the evil spirits in exchange for the fleeting power to be naughty—to harm an enemy, bewitch a neighbor's cow, or bed an otherwise unwilling partner.

There are many people in the world today (magicians and non-magicians alike) who believe quite literally that the above arrangement is the only spiritual game plan in town. It is certainly their right to do so; after all, for many of us this God/devil, heaven/hell, angel/demon morality play is the familiar foundation upon which the perversely comfortable "faith of our fathers" was built.

While I certainly do not wish to offend anyone's sincere spiritual beliefs (and I hold my hand up and swear, "Some of my best friends are Chrislemews!"), I must, however, be honest. I do not believe in such an all-good anthropomorphic god. Neither do I believe in an all-evil anthropomorphic devil. I don't believe in a heaven where I'll be rewarded for believing correctly or a hell where I'll be punished for my unbelief. In fact, I believe there is something terribly wrong and spiritually toxic with this entire picture—dangerously and tragically wrong—a wrongness that has plagued the Western psyche for millennia; a primitive and superstitious phantasm of the mind; a nightmare that has infected the human soul with the virus of fear and self-loathing; a cancerous curse that demands that every man, woman, and child surrender to the great lie that would make us believe that our very humanness makes us unclean and damned in the eyes of a wrathful deity.

Does my rejection of a too-literal interpretation of the scriptural worldview of the Chrislemews make me an atheist? For those who adhere too tightly to their doctrines, I guess it does—but it certainly does *not* from my point of view.[7] I most ardently believe in (indeed, I worship) a supreme consciousness that is the ultimate source of all manifest and unmanifest existence. I believe that you and I and every other monad of existence are components of the supreme consciousness. My morality (if you insist on calling it that) is based on my conviction that the ultimate nature of this super-existence is transcendently *Good*—a Good we can never adequately define with our words or understand with our meat brains—a Good so all-comprehensively infinite that there can be nothing outside of itself—*not even nothing.*

There can be no opposite of this great Good. The Goodness of supreme existence is spelled with the largest capital "G" imaginable. I call it the:

"Great G."

(There I go again, making up words. Well…get used to it, because I'm going to use this one a lot!)

This Great G swallows up the concept of duality. It neutralizes all concepts that remain so small that it is possible for them to have opposites—ideas such as a god who is so small and incomplete that there is an *outside-of-himself* where a pesky devil can go

---

7 After all, I can't be an atheist. I'm a Freemason!

running around causing trouble; ideas such as darkness and light; good little goods and evil little evils; little highs and little lows.

Perhaps the brains of our ancestors were not developed enough to grasp the idea of the Great Goodness of supreme existence. After all, in the ages when the Chrislemew and proto-Chrislemew doctrines were invented, our minds were yet unexpanded and unburdened by thoughts of gravity, or the speed of light, or the rotation of the Earth or its orbit of the sun, or black holes, or the nature of space-time. Perhaps back then it was impossible for us to wrap our minds around a reality that didn't spring solely from the primitive fear-based motivations of reward and punishment, pain and pleasure. Perhaps then—but not any longer!

After nearly forty years of magical study and practice, I've come to the conclusion that magick is magick. It is a spiritual art form by which we collect and direct a natural and neutral force whose source is the supreme intelligence—the supreme consciousness. In the right hands and under the right circumstances, the application of magick can be creative or destructive, helpful or harmful. It is not the magick is that is good or evil, or high or low—it is the magician.

No matter how pious and virtuous one may believe oneself to be—no matter how seemingly altruistic one's motives—no matter how precise and eloquently one executes the invocations to enlist the favor of God and the services of his angels, a magician who has not yet grasped this big picture and achieved a significant measure of spiritual maturity, mental stability, and purity of heart is not yet equipped to recognize relative good from relative evil. Like a marksman firing a powerful weapon in the dark, the naïve or superstitious magician is incapable of accurately hitting the mark or determining what magical actions will or will not be in his or her best interests. Conversely, if the magician is in touch with the Great G, there is no devil too evil, no angel too fallen, no demon too foul to be redeemed and pressed into the service of the Great Work.

And so, at the very beginning of my little book, I hereby confess that my title is a facetious and mischievous blind. It is with my tongue planted firmly in my cheek that I use the term "Low Magick" to describe the magical operations that follow. However, please don't think that by using the term I am being silly for silliness sake.

Many years ago, as a naïve and desperate young magician, I evoked Orobas, a demon from the Goetia,[8] for the purpose of turning around my impoverished and chaotic life circumstances—to save my family, to provide materially for my wife and child, and to give me the emotional stability to pursue the Great Work. In my naïve and inexperienced mind, it was an act of black magick—an encounter with the devil himself that I was prepared to perform against my teacher's wishes. In fact, when I told her I had become so desperate that I intended to go through with it, she flatly forbade it. When I asked her if she had ever performed such an operation, she said, "Certainly not! That's low magick."

In an act of magical disobedience, I did it anyway. I knew I had to. I had to succeed because the consequences of failure at that point in my life were unthinkable. I was fearful and clumsy. The operation almost immediately turned into a terrifying and traumatic comedy of errors that more resembled an industrial accident and a nervous breakdown than a magical ceremony. The climax of the ceremony was a life-and-death confrontation and struggle with the real demon responsible for my miserable situation—*me.*

---

8 *The Book of the Goetia of Solomon the King. Translated into the English Tongue by a Dead Hand and Adorned with Divers Other Matter Germane Delightful to the Wise, the Whole Edited, Verified, Introduced and Commented by Aleister Crowley.* Most recent edition with engraved illustrations of the spirits by M. L. Breton and foreword by Hymenaeus Beta (York Beach, ME: Samuel Weiser, 1996). Known as the *Lesser Key of Solomon,* it is the First Book of the Lemegeton (c. 1687). Translated by S. L. MacGregor Mathers (the "Dead Hand" referred to in the full title above). From the British Library Sloane Manuscripts nos. 2731 and 3648.

The whole crazy business seemed to pull out of my guts the very worst in me—my worst fears—the worst aspects of my character—my worst insecurities and feelings of shame and guilt. I didn't know it at the time, but that was exactly what was supposed to be happening. That's what Solomonic magick is all about. The worst in me was my problem. The worst in me was the demon. When it finally dawned on me that I had successfully evoked the demon, and I had the worst of me trapped in that magick Triangle, I had no alternative but to harness and redirect its monstrous power and give it new marching orders. From then on, that particular demon would be working for me rather than against me.

I'll spare you the details,[9] but suffice to say within minutes of concluding my bumbling act of low magick, a dramatic event occurred that set into motion a chain of events that, with breathtaking speed, accomplished everything I asked Orobas to deliver. But the real miracle was not the magical *quid pro quo* of a demon bent to obedience by the will of a magician, but the miracle of a magician who had redeemed a *better demon* of his nature. When the fiasco was over, I was a different person—a person who would save his family, provide materially for his wife and his child, and in the days and months and years ahead, clutch onto just enough emotional stability to pursue the Great Work.

In the first sentence of this chapter, I referred to Eliphas Lévi as "the great nineteenth-century esotericist." I did not call him a magician. Even though Monsieur Lévi is universally lauded as the father of modern high magick, he was not a practicing magician. He was a brilliant scholar, a holy man, a teacher, and a magical philosopher, but, with the exception of one curious necromantic experiment that he confessed was not at all successful, he did not practice magick.

---

9 I describe this incident in greater detail in several other places in my previously published works, especially *My Life with the Spirits: The Adventures of a Modern Magician* (York Beach, ME: Red Wheel/Weiser, 1999).

I *do* practice magick. In fact, I now view my entire life, waking and sleeping, to be a continuous magical operation. And so, gentle reader, for the duration of this book, the stories I shall tell of magical operations that I have actually *done* rather than just read about, *performed* rather than just discussed, *experienced* rather than just fantasized, and *executed* rather than merely mused upon—I will affectionately and unapologetically call acts of "low magick."

TWO

||||||||||||||||||||||||||||||||||||||||||||||||||||||||||||||||||||||||||||||||||||||||||||||||||||||||||||||||||

THE FORMULA OF SOLOMON

Give therefore to thy servant an understanding heart to
judge thy people and to discern between good and bad?

FIRST KINGS, CHAPTER 3, VERSE 9[1]

It may seem odd to you that I, as a man who more or less rejects the historicity of the Bible and most, if not all, of the Chrislemew view of spiritual reality, should spend my time praying to God, conjuring spirits, summoning demons, and communing with angels. Make no mistake, I do indeed believe in the magical reality of gods, archangels, angels, spirits, and demons, and for the purpose of some particular magical operations, I even embrace (albeit temporarily) the concept of a heaven filled with angels of high intelligence, and a hell filled with legions of dangerous demons. In fact, because I actually work with these characters in practical ways,

---

1 *The Holy Bible from Ancient Eastern Manuscripts.* Translated from Aramaic by George M. Lamsa (Philadelphia, PA: A.J. Holman Company, 1967), 378.

they present to me a far greater reality than they do for the average Chrislemew who simply tucks these concepts away in a corner of his or her brain where fanciful religious abstractions are stored.

As you will soon see, several of the stories in this book deal with my experiences with Solomonic magick or Goetia. Goetia is often vilified as the most striking example of low magick. Please understand right now that I do not intend to burden you with another rehash or a tiresome reprint of the text *Goetia*[2] with its seventy-two spirits and the traditional procedures used to conjure them. (There is a glut of books already on the market if that is what you need.) Rather, I hope by means of simple anecdotes and illustrations to gently acquaint you with the dynamics of this kind of magick— why it sometimes works, and why it sometimes doesn't. Moreover, it is my hope that when you have finished reading this little book, you will have a greater understanding of the sublime spiritual formula that underlies this kind of magical practice—a formula, when properly applied, that promises to the tenacious and courageous magician a greater measure of personal health, happiness, and enlightenment.

The formula of Solomonic magick is very simple and uses the character of King Solomon as the mythological archetype of the ideal magician. There are many stories and traditions about Solomon that come from sources other than the Bible. An important part of the mythology of Freemasonry revolves around a peculiar story of King Solomon and the building of his magnificent

---

2 *The Book of the Goetia of Solomon the King—Translated into the English Tongue by a Dead Hand and Adorned with Divers Other Matter Germane Delightful to the Wise, the Whole Edited, Verified, Introduced and Commented by Aleister Crowley* (Inverness, Scotland: Society for the Propagation of Religious Truth, Boleskine, Foyers, 1904). Known as the *Lesser Key of Solomon*, it is the First Book of the Lemegeton (c. 1687). Translated by S. L. MacGregor Mathers (the "Dead Hand" referred to in the full title above) from the British Library Sloane Manuscripts nos. 2731 and 3648. Most recent edition with engraved illustrations of the spirits by M. L. Breton and foreword by Hymenaeus Beta (York Beach, ME: Samuel Weiser, 1996).

temple—a story that is not found in the Bible. The Koran, the Talmud, and Ethiopian scriptures also abound with colorful tales of the great magician king who, because of his special relationship with God and his mastery of magick, could talk with animals, fly through the air on a magick carpet, and effect all manner of works and wonders, including his ability to enlist a labor force of demons and evil spirits to build the great Temple of God.

The likelihood that the biblical King Solomon probably never existed in empirical history should be of no concern to modern magicians, because the "formula" for doing this kind of magick isn't an aspect or product of history or religion but of the mythology and traditions that are attached to Solomon's name. The magical myth goes something like this:

When Solomon became king, his first job was to build a temple worthy to house the presence of the True and Living God Most High, something his father, David, hadn't been able to do. Before beginning the project, Solomon paused and thought things over and wisely came to the conclusion that he couldn't undertake such an important task without the blessing and guiding intelligence of God. In prayer, Solomon didn't ask for money or building materials or contractors; he simply asked for an "understanding heart."

How cool was that! It impressed God so much that Solomon was granted his request and given everything else to boot, including the divine secrets of how to magically summon the evil spirits of the world and (diverting them from their natural preoccupation with mischief) compel them to work for the good guys and help build the great temple.

On the surface, this spiritual worldview appears to be at odds with the Chrislemew doctrines we discussed in the preceding chapter. We've got God up above, and we've got demons down below, but it appears that's where the similarity ends. In fact, the whole format of Solomonic magick appears to be an incongruous mixture of high and low magick. The key to understanding this paradox lies with the person of Solomon himself.

Solomon represents a new kind of human being—a person who has broken free of the old ways of looking at God and our place in creation—a person whose consciousness has expanded beyond the prison universe of *good* gods and *evil* devils—a person who grasps the concept of a supreme consciousness so absolute that all forces and powers of creation (even those that to others appear evil and destructive) are pressed into service of the Great G Goodness.

A true "Solomon" confidently knows his or her place in this new understanding of the divine scheme of things. A true Solomon is a proactive full citizen of both heaven and hell. A true Solomon is, in fact, encouraged by the Great G God Almighty to conjure the devils and put them to work doing *good* things!

Are you confused? Don't be. You've just learned a fundamental secret of magick, and if you can free yourself from the old Chrislemew way of looking at things, you are well on the way to becoming a true Solomon yourself. Let me put it in less romantic terms.

The nature of existence is consciousness. We are conscious beings, each of us an integral part of the whole consciousness enchilada. There are levels of consciousness (and realities) above the one in which we normally function, and there are levels of consciousness below. As yogis, mystics, and adept magicians can attest, we can access the higher levels of consciousness in meditation or under other extraordinary circumstances. In those altered states we not only *realize* the oneness of the supreme consciousness, we *become* the oneness of the supreme consciousness. Ultimately, this transcendent state is our true and natural state of being, our true self; it is who we really are. It is the "heaven" where we dwell when we have fulfilled our adventures pretending we are somehow disconnected from the supreme consciousness. Our ascent into higher consciousness is Solomon's prayer to God—Solomon *going up* to be in the presence of Deity.

However, because most of us have not yet played out our adventures of dreaming we are separate entities, we can abide these exalted states for only fleeting seconds before once again descending to the middle-muddled world of the rational mind, which in turn is supported by the "infernal" world of matter and energy at the lowest end of the consciousness scale. It is a place where the blind forces of nature (if left uncontrolled and undirected) happily discharge their wild energy in explosive flashes that surge through the streets and sewers of our souls along the paths of least resistance. From our narrow, middle-world perspective, these blind forces appear to be destructive and evil. However, when they are harnessed and directed by an intelligence that is in tune with the highest levels of consciousness, they are transformed into organized units of the constructive power—loyal servants dutifully grunting and straining to perform all the heavy lifting in the universe. These are the demons who build the Temple of God—demons Solomon *draws up* from hell so he might bind them to work under his enlightened and organized direction.

For the magician, archangels, angels, spirits, intelligences, and demons are merely colorful metaphors for the cascading hierarchy of all the natural forces and energies of the universe. This is the secret of Solomon. Once we've really pounded it into our heads, we recognize that we, too, have our unique place in the universe. Proactively operating halfway between the *above* and the *below*, we are poised to connect *with* and become charged *by* forces of the stratum of consciousness above us so that we may connect with, master, and direct the forces in the stratum beneath us.

For the magician, the energy flow of the Solomonic formula moves perpetually upward. The magician's consciousness rises to connect with the divine consciousness (earth up to heaven) to become attuned with the divine perfection; and the demon is made to rise up (hell up to earth) to become controlled and directed by the magician. From the demon's point of view, the magician is God, and as long as the magician's link with the "above" is true and sure, so too is the demon's link with the magician.

The reason this kind of low magick has earned such an evil reputation is because we so often hear of the terrible consequences to the life and sanity of the magician who violates this simple upward-flowing formula. I speak specifically of cases where in the course of the operation the spirit convinces the magician to strike some sort of bargain—a *quid pro quo*, perhaps a gift or sacrifice in exchange for service. *"I'll bring you a nice shiny penny... but you've got to kill the vicar!"* Ask any Solomonic magician; he or she will most likely tell you the first thing a spirit will attempt to extract from you is a bargain of some kind, or an amendment to your original request. It is also the last thing you should consider doing.

In all fairness to the poor infernal spirit, such haggling is a perfectly understandable characteristic of its unredeemed nature to try to negotiate itself free from your control. After all, it's been doing that in one way or another your entire life—otherwise you wouldn't be lacking the specific thing the spirit can provide you!

But what if the formula is breached? What happens if, instead of raising the spirit up to the magician's level, the magician descends to the demon's level? Shouldn't a competent magician be able to handle that?

My answer is yes. A competent magician, a true Solomon, *can* handle that, but one must question his or her motives for setting out to do so. Is the object of the operation to cause some change to occur in hell? Or is the object of the operation to cause some change to occur in the magician's life here on earth? If the answer is the latter (and I can't imagine it being otherwise), then it is probably wisest to bring the demon up to where its work is to be done, rather than casting oneself down to the hell of *status quo* where the spirit lounges comfortably in your screwed-up life-as-usual. The worker's daily labor is done on the factory floor, not at the union hall.

A year or two ago, a young man wrote me a letter asking if there was some way for him to use a black mirror or other magical method so that he might actually visit the realm where the Goetic entities dwell. I was in an odd mood, so I wrote him the following response, which I hope he took in the *spirit* it was intended:

Dear (name withheld),

A partial answer to your question would be another question; that is… "What makes you think you are not already visiting the realm where the Goetic spirits dwell?"

I'm not kidding. If you wish to explore the realm where some of these fragments of consciousness dwell, I suggest that tonight, as an experiment, you go visit the sleaziest saloon in the roughest part of town about an hour before closing. Every untamed manifestation of the denizens of your Nephesh[3] (the real spirits of your Goetia) will be poised to appear before your eyes.

Buy them a round of drinks. They will toast you. Join them in their libations. Keep drinking and talking with them until you start to think their crude and bigoted jokes are really funny and you begin to actually agree with their views of politics and religion. Breathe in the infernal incense of the cigarette smoke. Inhale the sacred perfume of body odor, spilled beer, and urinal cakes. Become one with the consciousness of the room. There! You are visiting hell on earth.

---

3 According to Qabalists, the Nephesh (animal soul) is the lowest of the four parts of the human soul. Above the Nephesh is the *Ruach* (the intellect), above that, the *Neshamah* (soul intuition), then, at the top, the *Chiah* (life force).

Granted, you might have the magician's presence of mind
(Ruach)[4] to jot down some names and phone numbers and
thus arrange to have one of these beasties meet you tomorrow in the sober light of day so that you might hire him
or her to mow your lawn, paint your house, or clean your
septic tank. On the other hand, you could surrender your
Ruach completely and stumble home with one of your new
Goetic friends for the prospect of a vomit-covered stab at
intimacy (and then wake up in the morning to find yourself robbed, infected, or worse, looking every bit the demon
yourself).

And so my friend, to answer your question specifically
and on a practical level, yes, it is possible to visit the realm
where the Goetic spirits dwell, and you won't need an ex-
pensive black obsidian mirror to do it. Choose the seal[5] of
the Goetic spirit you wish to visit. Draw it carefully on a
tiny piece of paper. Take it with you to that saloon tonight
at midnight and swallow it with your first strong drink.

Bon voyage!

The formal technique of Solomonic magick is simple, almost intuitive. First, I need to have an "object of my operation," a change
I wish to effect in my life, e.g., "I want Mary, the girl next door, to
fall in love with me."

I start by creating a circle of sacred space in a convenient area of
my home or garden. I draw out a triangle on the floor before my
circle and do whatever I think necessary to contact and invoke the
blessing and presence of the Great G in the likeness and character
of the deity of my choice. (I will discuss the importance of invo-

4 Ibid.
5 See chapter 13.

cation and the choice of one's deity in later chapters.) Once I am confident that my motives are in harmony with the divine order and that I am the living representative of the Great G, I use that authority to summon a demon from the "infernal regions" into the magick Triangle. Once the demon appears (either tangibly or in my mind's eye), I give it its marching orders: "Cause Mary to fall in love with me." Then I set it loose to do my bidding.

Sounds corny and melodramatic, doesn't it? It *is* corny and melo-dramatic! It's supposed to be corny and melodramatic. That's the romance and charm of the Solomonic magick art form. But it is easy to perform, and if all the factors of the formula are in place, it will work. However, it is likely to work in ways you might not expect.

In the case of our example, let's not forget that Mary has a di-vine—and potentially omnipotent—Will of her own. Unless *she* somehow recognizes the cosmic correctness of falling in love with me—unless she cooperates in this operation, I'm going to remain eternally snubbed. It is likely that Mary is not in love with me because I'm currently not the kind of person Mary is ready to fall in love with. It's not Mary who will have to change, it's me. If it is truly my Will to be Mary's lover, I will have to be transformed into the kind of person with whom Mary falls in love.

Chances are, in the days and weeks following my evocation—in the ordinary course of *my* life—under circumstances that might appear to have nothing to do with my magical operation—I will be called upon to seriously play the part of a magician, and to play that part well. As a matter of fact, it is likely that (as the result of my Goetic evocation) I will find myself involved in some kind of adventurous struggle.

I've often said that the only thing I can change with magick is my-self. I believe that. Whatever changes I wish to effect with magick, the first and only thing that will be *directly* changed by my magical operation will be *me*. Once I am changed, then the *new changed me* will then somehow affect or attract the desired object of my operation. However, we seldom know in advance what changes we'll need to undergo to become that new person. Furthermore, it is a cold hard fact of life that change often comes as the result of trauma. Perhaps Mary is the kind of girl who can only fall in love with a blind man, or an amputee, or a Republican.

Funny thing about demons. If you're a Solomon, they make wonderful employees. But if you're not, they make terrible bosses. They are easy to call up. They run amok in our lives as the frenzied menagerie of our own uncontrolled and undirected energies. When we willfully put one to work for us, we are in essence saying to the cosmos of consciousness, "I will conquer and redeem this demon from hell, and the battle will take the form of a character-building adventure. The adventure will transform the demon into a loyal and worthy employee, and transform me into a new and different person—a masterful person—the kind of person the object of my magical operation happens to—the kind of person Mary falls in love with."

So bring it on, the magician shouts. Let the adventure begin!

THE MAGICIAN[6]

O Lord, deliver me from hell's great fear and gloom!
Loose thou my spirit from the larvae of the tomb!
I seek them in their dread abodes without affright:
On them will I impose my will, the law of light.

I bid the night conceive the glittering hemisphere.
Arise, O sun, arise! O moon, shine white & clear!

---

6 *The Magician*, translated from Eliphas Lévi's version of the famous hymn. See chapter VII of my book *Angels, Demons & Gods of the New Millennium* (York Beach, ME: Red Wheel/Weiser, 1997), 151–166.

I seek them in their dread abodes without affright:
  On them will I impose my will, the law of light.

Their faces and their shapes are terrible and strange.
  These devils by my might to angels I will change.
  These nameless horrors I address without affright:
  On them will I impose my will, the law of light.

These are the phantoms pale of mine astonied view,
  Yet none but I their blasted beauty can renew;
  For to the abyss of hell I plunge without affright:
  On them will I impose my will, the law of light.

||||||||||||||||||||||||||||||||||||||||||||||||||||||||||||||||||||||||||||||||||||||||||||||||||||||||||

THREE

THE LAW OF ATTRACTION, THE POWER OF INTENT & MY DATE WITH LINDA KAUFMAN

Intent is the mechanics through which spirit transforms itself into material reality.

DEEPAK CHOPRA,
The Spontaneous Fulfillment of Desire

In the last few years, we've heard a lot about the Law of Attraction and the Power of Intent. At the risk of being shunned and ridiculed by the more hard-core wizards of the occult community, I have to confess my deep and abiding respect for the works of Louise Hay, Deepak Chopra, and Dr. Wayne Dyer, among others, for bringing to a wider audience of seekers the fundamental secrets of true magick in ways that are understandable and acceptable to people of all spiritual backgrounds.

Perhaps you don't think that such fluffy New Age pundits could actually be tossing around the supreme secret of the ages on public television sandwiched between cooking shows and reruns of *Masterpiece Theatre*... but they are! Magick may be the science and art of causing change to occur in conformity with Will, but the mechanism of that Will can be at least partially described by the single word "intent."

Magical theory suggests that everything in the universe is the product of intent. I wouldn't dare to attempt to prove this vast and unprovable statement (and gods forbid I would dare open the absurd "intelligent design" can of imaginary worms). I will, however, not hesitate to point out how many *things* in our shared reality—objects, inventions, events, ideas, religious and political movements, even our view of time—can demonstrably be the direct and unambiguous products of intention. Take this book as an example:

It is my intent to communicate a few of my thoughts and experiences concerning magick to as many people as possible; it is also my intent to earn some money in order to help keep a roof over my head, and sustain a modicum of self-respect for myself and my family as I look to the fast-approaching years of my dotage.[1]

It is my publisher's intent (among other things) to provide a quality literary product in such a manner as to make the maximum profit from the minimum expenditure, and to provide information and entertainment to the book-buying public (especially those individuals whose interests are in harmony with the publisher's philosophies and interests). Furthermore, it is the publisher's intent to keep his or her family of employees, subcontractors, printers, distributors, suppliers, etc., gainfully employed and contributing to the intended support and well-being of *their* families, communities, etc.

---

1 Believe me, writing occult books is an insanely bad way to get rich quick.

As the reader (I am assuming), it is your intent (among other things) to enrich your life with the knowledge and ideas presented in this book, and to use this information and insight for your own intended applications.

Magical intent has much in common with what we normally associate with the concept of willpower. It is, however, something much greater than the teeth-gritting power of concentration to *force* something to happen that was otherwise not going to happen. Magical intent is more a matter of "seeing" what you truly want so clearly that your vision (indeed, your *love of the vision*) creates a living entity. Faced with the birth of this new cosmic citizen on the *creative* plane, the universe has no alternative but to rearrange conditions on the *material* plane to accommodate the complete manifestation of this now-inevitable object or event.

You may find this hard to believe, but I learned the secret power of magical intent when I was six years old. The inspiration for my operation was my kindergarten classmate, Linda Kaufman. She was the most beautiful girl at George Washington Carver Elementary School in Lakewood, California. I always arranged to sit near her for rhythm band and finger painting. She seemed to enjoy my antics, especially my sophisticated ability to bark like a sea lion. I also had the pity factor working for me because the first few months of my kindergarten year I was forced by a serious hip condition to walk with the aid of crutches.[2]

I was insanely in love with her and each night as I lay in bed I fantasized how I would take her to the movies on a real grown-up date. I correct myself: It was not a fantasy. It was a vision of a perfect moment of *love*—a perfect vision of love given—and of love received.

---

2 When I was three years old, I was diagnosed with Perthes' disease in my right hip. Perthes' is a serious bone malady that crumbles the topmost part of the thigh. In order to prevent complete disintegration of my hip socket, my doctor ordered me off my feet. When I started school, I was required to use crutches for the first few months. By the age of fourteen I was pronounced free of the disease.

For months I rehearsed the scene in my imagination. I would be dressed in a suit and tie. I would somehow drive to her house and pick her up. I'd meet her parents. Her father would invite me into his den and offer me a cocktail (like they drank on the television show, *Topper*). Then Linda would appear in a pretty new dress and we'd drive off to the movie theatre. I'd buy us some popcorn. We'd find seats near the front and share our popcorn and giggle. Then, when the lights went down and the film began, she would take my arm (because I'd be too shy and polite to do it myself) and put it around her shoulders, and she and I would snuggle close for the whole movie.

It was a lovely dream, and I was determined to make it happen. During Christmas vacation in 1954, I approached my mother in the kitchen and told her I wanted to take Linda Kaufman to the movies. I ordered her to call Linda's parents "right now" and arrange everything. It was a bold move. I was conjuring a dangerous demon. My mother could be unpredictably violent and cruelly abusive. It was such an odd little demand, however, that I think it took her completely off balance. I didn't have the slightest doubt that she would obey my command. She stared at me for a moment, then picked up the phone and called Linda's mother. They laughed and gossiped for what seemed like hours. When she hung up, it was a done deal.

New Year's Day 1955 was a Sunday—the perfect day for Linda and me to see the new biblical epic, *The Silver Chalice*.[3] Mom and my older brother Marc (he and his date would be our chaperones) waited in the car while I, dressed smartly in my Sunday school sports jacket and clip-on tie, knocked on the door of the Kaufman residence. Her dad answered and invited me into his den and told me to sit down.

---

3 Warner Brothers, released Christmas Day, 1954; starring Paul Newman, Virginia Mayo, and Jack Palance.

"Would you like something to drink?"

I couldn't believe this was happening. He poured us each a heavy highball glass of ginger ale and ice. I'd never tasted ginger ale before. Was this a cocktail? Linda soon appeared with her mother and spun around to show off her new dress. I was sure the ginger ale was taking effect. Everything, almost to the last detail, was happening exactly as I envisioned—and it didn't stop there.

At the theater, with my brother and his date following discreetly behind us, I bought popcorn and Linda and I found our seats near the front. We giggled and munched, and when the lights dimmed and the big Warner Brothers shield beamed at us from the silver screen, Linda Kaufman, my goddess, the love of my life, grabbed my arm and put it around her shoulders, where it remained locked in sweaty, painful ecstasy for the next two hours and twenty-two minutes.

At that moment, I knew that my mind, my dreams had the power to make things happen. I knew there was some kind of living intelligence that hears the yearnings of my heart—a being—a god with the power to bring into reality anything I imagine—anything I intend. However, it would take me the better part of the next fifty years to understand that the nature of that power is *Love*, and that without that vital ingredient in the recipe, my magick would always fall short of perfection.

FOUR

||||||||||||||||||||||||||||||||||||||||||||||||||||||||||||||||||||||||||||||||||||||||||||||||||||||||||||||||||||||||

FAMILY SECRETS

In parts of Melanesia, where matriliny is the rule, magic is inherited from father to son; in Wales it seems that mothers handed it down to sons, while fathers bequeathed it to the daughters. In societies where voluntary secret societies for men play an important role, the association of magicians and the secret society usually overlap.

MARCEL MAUSS,
A General Theory of Magic

Some people in the magical community place a great deal of importance on their magical ancestry. This is not surprising because the romance and mythos of our spiritual art is certainly enhanced by the thought that we might in fact be a special breed set apart from ordinary people[1] by the very blood in our veins. I believe that in and of itself, this attitude can be harmless enough. After all, who of us wouldn't like to think that we are (even by tradition)

---

1 "Muggles," as J. K. Rowling, creator of the wildly popular Harry Potter books, might call them.

descended from a Merlin or a Morgan La Fey, a Cagliostro or an Aleister Crowley? Taken too seriously, however, such preoccupation with magical bloodlines can easily seduce us into blindly abandoning our common sense and embracing a form of magical elitism as foolish and dangerous as any other *name-your-own supremacy*.

Please don't misunderstand me. I fully recognize the fact that a few of us actually have parents who studied and practiced magick or witchcraft, and that they too may have had parents who did the same. For most of us, however, the "magick" we've inherited from our parents or grandparents is something less overtly magical than that determined by our family's participation in generational covens, satanic cults, or secret initiatory societies. In fact, I believe that we can discover more about the magical "blood" of our ancestors by simply examining their lives and characters than we can by analyzing their professed spiritual interests.

I'd wager that if each of us gave it a little thought, we could find the magician in our parents and grandparents and be able to trace that magick (whether for good or ill) to our own lives and personalities. I certainly can. As a matter of fact, if you wish to truly become a wise and well-rounded magician, you will sooner or later have to come to terms with both the good and evil locked in the DNA of your own family secrets.

With your permission, I would like to share a couple of stories from my magical family tree. Perhaps you will be able to see some parallels in your own life. If not, you might at least learn a bit more about me.

My mother[2] was a fundamentalist Christian who took perverse pride in the fact that she did *not* know—nor did she care to learn— the history or tenets of Christianity (even her own brand). She did not read (let alone study) the Bible. "Childlike faith" was the sole

---

2 Lucinda McConnell-DuQuette-Lees (1913–2007).

virtue she boasted would get her into heaven. In her mind, curiosity and education would only open the door to the devil's wiles and tempt her to doubt the one true way of blind faith that was pounded into her as a child growing up on the unforgiving prairie of western Nebraska. This devotional focus could have been a powerful spiritual tool in her life if it were not for the fact that there was not an *object* for her devotion. She did not seem particularly devoted to Jesus or interested in the spiritual significance of the passion of his life. She was thoroughly content with the concept that if she unquestioningly believed that he, as an historical character, died on the cross, came back to life three days later, and then he flew up into the sky forty days after that, then she would go to heaven—and everyone who *didn't* believe those things would be justly punished in a blazing hell for eternity. Even as a child, I believe she delighted more in the thought of the damnation of unbelievers than in the promise of sweet salvation for believers.

Belief in such doctrines isn't necessarily cause for criticism or condemnation. Indeed, I've known many people that hold very similar religious beliefs—people with loving hearts who possess deep compassion for their families, friends, neighbors, and communities. But with all respect due to the woman who brought me into this dimension, I am sad to report that my mother was not one of these people. For her, this small exercise in intolerant religious absolutism only freed her to focus her entire energies upon the one and only object of her true spiritual devotion—herself.

She was supernaturally psychic and possessed a power of personality so magnetic that it captured and dominated everyone around her. This made her initially attractive to others, and in social environments, very popular. Time after time during her ninety-four-year incarnation, casual acquaintances became her unsuspecting victims, falling voluntarily under her spell only to later find themselves stung, paralyzed and hopelessly entangled in her web of emotional servitude. She was a charismatic dictator who ironically had no master plan other than to create explosions of emotional turmoil in the lives of those around her and then to draw energy from all that turmoil. After thirty-three years of suffering her soul-draining dramas, my father died at the age of sixty-two. Twenty-three years later, the same fate awaited a second husband. Her magick touch would also prove fatal to the health, careers, marriages, and relationships of scores of relatives, friends, and well-meaning strangers.

Ironically, she had (at times) a great sense of humor—and humor is the inheritance from her I most treasure. Humor continues to help me cope with and (hopefully) transmute the darker magick she bequeathed me. Here are a few passages from the eulogy I delivered at her funeral. I may sound a bit disrespectful in the short clip below, but the pastor and congregation of her church certainly didn't think so. They knew my mother too well. The laughter in the sanctuary was a healthy discharge of emotion for all of us.

FROM: A SON'S EULOGY

Christ Presbyterian Church,
Lakewood, California, January 26, 2008

I'm sure not all mothers are vampires, but mine was. I sucked her milk for less than a year; then she sucked my blood for the next fifty-nine. Up to a point, I think it's part of the natural order of things. We all live off each other in one way or another. If someone really needs to be nourished with my energy, I'm happy to "bleed" a little for them, but I really resent it when they don't really "drink" my blood but instead spill it all over the floor. I'm sad to say in her ninety-four years Mom spilled a lot of people's blood all over the floor.

Please don't get me wrong. Mom loved *people*... but she hated all other living things. You'd never catch her petting a dog or stroking a cat. She strove to kill all insects both inside and outside of the house. She didn't even care too much for flowers because of the chance they might harbor an insect.

You never wanted to take her to a restaurant to which you ever intended to return. She ran waiters and waitresses ragged... and if she didn't like the food, she would often call them to the table, take the food out of her mouth and say, "Honey... look at this... would you eat that?" She would then try to get them to eat some of it before sending it back. Toward the end of the meal, she always loudly announced (within earshot of the haggard waitress) that she didn't believe in tipping.

She *always* stole the napkins.

To say she was strong-willed and self-centered would be a colossal understatement. If I were to use the title of a popular song to describe the character of this amazing person, it would have to be Frank Sinatra's "My Way"!

As a matter of fact, when she was in her late seventies, she demonstrated how true this was by causing herself and her entire party to be kicked out of a Frank Sinatra concert in Long Beach because she refused to stop loudly chatting with her friends during his performance.

Sadly, I must give her mixed reviews as far as her parenting skills were concerned. She subscribed to the old-school philosophy that states a mother should never whip a child unless she is red-in-the-face in the throes of a violent blind rage and completely *out of control.* These beatings were perhaps tame compared to some stories of abuse. Once, however, as I struggled to escape a paddling, she missed her mark and hit me in the head with the edge of the wooden paddle. I guess it scared her pretty badly to see me stunned blind and bouncing off the furniture.

But I'm all grown up now ... and have forgotten all about it.

Because I was the second-born child, I personally escaped many of the more severe and damaging effects her maternal learning curve visited upon my older brother Marc in the six years of his life before I was born.

But Marc's all grown up now too ... and I'm sure has forgotten all about it ...

Yes, Lucinda Myrtle DuQuette *was* quite a character—strong-willed, charismatic, wicked, and unforgettable. A few months before she died, I wrote her this little poem.

Perhaps we were neighbors.
Perhaps we were kin.
Perhaps we were husband and wife.
Perhaps we were friends.
Perhaps we were foes.
Perhaps we took each other's life.

No matter the bonds
We bring from the past,
Or what we once were to each other,
Whether parent or spouse,
Sister or brother,
This time around you're our mother.

So as this part of our lives
Draws near to a close,
And the stage soon will be set for another,
Let's kiss and let's laugh, and set fire to the past,
And forgive and forget one another.

My father was a different kind of magician altogether. He was a quiet and moody Scorpio given to bouts of depression. He liked to drink during the years before I was born, but Mom's willingness to drive to his favorite after-work watering hole and physically pull him off his barstool and out to the car put an end to that. Dad didn't talk much about his parents and family, other than to say he had one sister and three half-sisters, all older than he. To my knowledge, he never met any of his grandparents. His father came from France; his mother came from England. She'd been married once before and had three girls from that union. Her father was an inspector for Scotland Yard who died during the events of Queen Victoria's Golden Jubilee. The only thing we know about Grandma DuQuette's mother was a story that I find somewhat unnerving—something that *my* mother didn't tell me until a week or so before she died in 2007. I was almost sixty years old when I heard the tale. I now know why she waited.

My father was born and raised in Los Angeles, but had traveled to western Nebraska in the late 1930s to drill exploratory oil wells. He met my mother-to-be (a waitress at a diner) and they married in the little town of Chapel, Nebraska, in 1940. When the newlyweds returned home to California, my father was stunned to discover that while he had been away, his father was dead and buried,[3] and his mother lay dying in a hospital. When they visited the poor woman, she asked to talk alone with her new daughter-in-law.

She asked my mother-to-be if she planned to have children. When Mom answered in the affirmative, the old woman pleaded with her to reconsider. "Don't have his children. We are cursed! There is evil in our blood." She then tearfully confessed that her own mother was a "witch."

---

3 Dad's sisters refused to reveal his father's burial site.

Now, I think here I must pause and point out for this woman born in the late 1800s, the word "witch" did not refer to a person who wholesomely embraced the life-affirming, earth-centered worship of today's Neopagan movement. Instead, it referred to someone who delighted in doing evil things for evil's sake.

She then went on to relate how her mother fed on the hate and fear and misery of others—how she would sit on the steps of her London flat and curse passersby, especially pregnant women, then later delight in reports of their miscarriages and deaths during childbirth. She poisoned dogs and cats. She spread vile rumors about neighbors and relatives for no other purpose than that of ruining lives. So hated and feared was she in the neighborhood that no child was allowed to play with her children, and if not for the fact that her husband was a policeman, the family would have been run out of the neighborhood.

None of my father's four sisters had any children, perhaps warded off by tales of evil blood. My mother, on the other hand, was a different creature altogether. When I asked her if Grandma DuQuette's warning hadn't scared her, she coldly answered, "No. Where would you and Marc be if I had listened? I wasn't going to let that old witch tell me what to do."

I think in this case Mom's magick served a very good purpose. It dug its heels in and triumphed over fear and superstition (albeit with a heavy dose of fear and superstition of its own). Even though my father wouldn't live the luckiest of lives, even though my brother and I have had our share of ups and downs, I don't believe that any of the DuQuettes who sprang from this strange woman's loins are cursed with anything more sinister than our own human shortcomings. However, this unsettling story now makes me recall that for my entire childhood, whenever I did something my mother disapproved of, she would shake her finger at me and tell me, in deadly earnest, that I was "possessed with the devil."

I must also confess that at times I can be possessed by a disturbing, dark, and hateful nature. When I perceive that I've been wronged—when someone cuts me off on the freeway, when I hear of or observe the mistreatment of other people or animals or my country or my planet—I become so overwhelmed with the most monstrous bloodcurdling images of what I would do to such people if they were at my mercy in some fantasy torture chamber that I have to use every weapon in my mystical arsenal to force myself back to calm sanity. At times like this, I am mindful of a great-grandmother who poisoned people's pets and delighted in the news of miscarriages.

For all appearances, this curse skipped my father. In fact, my father was blessed with a most kind and noble character. It was obvious he stayed married to Mom for the welfare and safety of Marc and me. His spirituality was centered upon a simple belief in a generic "Supreme Being" (after all—he was a Freemason[4]) and in the fundamental goodness of human beings.[5] He took the time to instill in his sons a confidence that we could do anything we put our minds to. He taught us the magick of dreams and imagination, and that it was possible to work to make our dreams come true.

Like a good Scorpio Freemason, he taught us by means of magical secrets. So now, after you have patiently endured my ponderous Freudian excursions into my mother's sorcery, I finally come to the true *family secrets* the title of this chapter initially promised you.

Dad's library contained a number of Masonic books, many illustrated with exotic, mystic symbols. When my brother and I asked

---

4 In most countries, Freemasons must profess belief in a Supreme Being.

5 Freemasons are also taught that "... a fund of science and industry is implanted in man for the best, most salutary and most beneficent purposes." This doctrine is in striking opposition to the Christian doctrines of Original Sin and the Total Depravity of Man.

what they meant, he would only tease us by saying, "It's a secret. If you want, when you grow up you can try to join the Masons and find out." He gently instilled in us both an awe and respect for secret knowledge. So when I was faced with the normal problems of growing up, I could go to Dad and he would give me a magick "secret" to dealing with them. These were secrets not to be shared with anyone else—not Mom; not my brother; no one! My brother and I were unaware at the time that the other was also getting his own secrets from Dad. Years after his death we compared notes and discovered that, while similar, each of our "secrets" had been uniquely composed.[6]

It's been many years since Dad passed away. I don't think he would mind if I'd share just a couple of the magical secrets that have helped me throughout the years.

- The first secret was not a secret *per se*; it was a commandment, a prime directive: "Your name is a magick name. Never change your name or the spelling of your name." I don't know why he named me Lon Milo, but one of my earliest memories of Dad was his insistence that he chose my name very carefully, that it was a magick name, and that I was never to change it, never to change the spelling or the capitalization. I continue to obey the prime directive.[7]

- *The Secret to falling asleep at night* was the first bona fide secret Dad taught me. It was a two-part secret, very simple (but I could tell no one how I do it). First, I was to say my prayers. Now, Dad was practically an agnostic, and God to him was a generic cosmic abstraction. He did not encourage me to em-

---

6 Please see appendix 1 for my brother Marc's own mystical story about Dad.

7 Qabalists might observe that when the letters of my name are replaced with Hebrew letters Lon Milo DuQuette enumerates to 444, and that my initials, LMD, spell the Hebrew letter Lamed.

brace Jesus or the Old Testament Jehovah, or indeed anything other than a supremely good *What-It-Is*. Nevertheless, it was important that before I go to sleep I should acknowledge Deity and thank it for the blessings of my life and ask for its continued protection, guidance, and blessing upon everything I do. He said the best prayer was one that just came out of my own heart, but if I couldn't make up a prayer of my own, the Lord's Prayer would work until I got the hang of it.

After saying my prayer, I was to relax and make up an imaginary adventure (with me as the main character) about anything that pleased me—the more fanciful the better. There was only one rule to this part of the secret: each night's adventure must include me doing at least one thing that is *impossible* to do in real life. I had to think of a new impossible act every night. I didn't know why, but I instinctively knew that this was one of the coolest things in the world you could encourage a kid to do.

· *The Secret to stopping nightmares* was perhaps the most overtly magical of Dad's secrets. Like most kids, I had my share of childhood nightmares. One night when I was about seven years old I woke up screaming and crying. It seems a monster had just eaten my brother Marc and that it had hold of my foot. Without turning on the light, Dad came into my room and sat on the bed. He told me everything was okay and that everybody had bad dreams now and again. He encouraged me to lie back down, but I refused to put my head on the same spot on the pillow where the bad dream came from. He then said the most curious thing. "No. You *want* to go back into the dream and make the monster go away." He then told me that whenever I am uncomfortable in a dream, I only have to pronounce my own name backwards, "NOL," and the monster or the problem would disappear. I trusted Dad, so I put my head back on the nightmare pillow and tried to re-create the dreaded moment. Sure enough—I was back in the dream with my foot in the monster's mouth. I spoke the magick word, NOL! The monster opened its mouth in fear and it dissolved into thin air. I was very impressed with my new secret. I would use it countless times. Furthermore, once I learned I could take control of my dreams, I learned I could "go" places in dreams and even live out some of those "impossible" feats of wonder. This is a skill that is very important to a magician. It is also very important to be able to resolve a problem in its own dimension rather than trying to run away from it by escaping into another.

• *The Secret of learning* was a simple affirmation that I was to say under my breath as I walked to school each morning: *"The Secret of learning is to do the best I can at all times; and always do a little better than I think I can."* I wish I could say this made me a model student, but I cannot. I will say, however, that I can't begin to imagine how terribly bad a student I could have been without this bit of morning encouragement.

I cannot escape that fact that both my parents were major factors in the equation that produced the magician Lon Milo DuQuette. As Constance and I raised our son, Jean-Paul, I was very mindful of object lessons I learned from my own parents' strengths and weaknesses. Our unique "family secrets" we've passed along to him he now shares in his own way with his own son, and so it goes.

How are things in your family?

|||||||||||||||||||||||||||||||||||||||||||||||||||||||||||||||||||||||||||||||||||||||||||||||||||||||||||||||||||

MY PLANETARY TALISMANS[1]

*This is the excellent foppery of the world, that, when we are sick in fortune—
often the surfeit of our own behavior—we make guilty of our disasters the sun,
the moon, and the stars: as if we were villains by necessity; fools by heavenly
compulsion; knaves, thieves, and treachers, by spherical predominance;
drunkards, liars, and adulterers, by an enforced obedience of planetary
influence; and all that we are evil in, by a divine thrusting on: an admirable
evasion of whoremaster man, to lay his goatish disposition to the charge of a star!*

SHAKESPEARE, *King Lear*

As a magician for last thirty-five years or so, I have, by means both
conventional and forbidden, endeavored to cause changes to occur in my life in conformity with what I have perceived to be my
Will. I say "perceived to be my Will" because it is not until one has
developed a significant level of illumination that one can with any
degree of certainty know what one's Will really is.

---

1 Partially excerpted from my foreword to the third revised limited edition of Israel
Regardie's *The Complete Golden Dawn System of Magic* (Reno, NV: New Falcon
Publications, 2008), 37–41.

Please don't assume that just because I have practiced magick for such a long time that I possess an unclouded vision of my true Will or that I consider myself an illuminated master. I do not. What I do possess, after all this time, is a great deal of magical experience; and experience is (or at least can be) the breeding ground of wisdom. Naturally, that potentiality disintegrates if I can't accurately recall and evaluate these experiences so that I might apply their lessons to the present state of my magical development. For this reason, I believe it is vitally important for magicians to keep a written record of their exploits. As I mentioned earlier, in order to write this book, I have dug deep into dusty boxes and storage bins to extract and organize the buried chronicles of my magical adventures and misadventures.

For me, reviewing old magical diaries is never a pleasant experience. Every time I open and read one of my ancient journals, I am paralyzed by a combination of nauseating embarrassment and amazement. I grit my teeth and squirm as I relive the events, the thoughts, delusions, and presumptions that occupied that shallow, self-centered, naïve, ego-blinded young fool who gawked back at me from the mirrors of yesterday. My singular consolation is the fact that I've survived to rejoice, "Thank God I'm not like *that* any longer!"

Painful as the experience is, reviewing my magical records affords me the opportunity to chart the general trajectory of my spiritual evolution. I have even been able, in several instances, to pinpoint the exact minute my magical efforts (high or low) have actually caused change to occur in conformity with my Will—times that have dramatically altered the course of my life, and the lives of others. In fact, at this very moment, *you* are reading the words on this page as the result of a magical operation I set in motion thirty-five years ago.

About a year before my traumatic evocation of the demon Orobas,[2] I was enmeshed in what I will politely describe as a crisis in my life. I was twenty-six years old, married, with a two-year-old son. I was desperately trying to wean myself from a very unhealthy career as a musician/recording artist, and struggling to bring some semblance of stability and direction to my life. Several years prior to this, to address an intense spiritual hunger, I entered the initiatory world of the Western mysteries—specifically the degree work of the *Rosicrucian Order, AMORC, The Traditional Martinist Order (TMO)*, and the *Builders of the Adytum (B.O.T.A.)*.

As fascinating as my studies were, they were just that—studies. My life needed changing. I didn't want to merely study magick; I wanted to *perform* magick. But what kind of magick? I had heard some pretty scary things about the evils of magick, so I was desperate to find a safe place to start.

Early in January 1975, in an old and stuffy little occult bookstore in North Long Beach, I purchased *How to Make and Use Talismans*[3] by Israel Regardie.[4] I trusted Regardie, having read several of his classic magical texts. This little book, however, was different. It was actually a how-to book of practical magick. Regardie's sane and straightforward explanation of the fundamentals of talismanic magick instantly dispelled my superstitious doubts. His generous offering of charts, diagrams, and illustrations (which I promptly copied and pasted into my magical diary) made it a treasure-trove of easy-to-use information. I couldn't wait to graduate from student to

---

2 See chapter 1.

3 Originally published by Sangreal. Most recent revised edition by Thorsons Publishers, 1983.

4 Israel Regardie (1907–1985), born Francis Israel Regudy, was personal secretary to occultist Aleister Crowley in the 1920s. He was arguably one of the twentieth century's most influential voices perpetuating the legacies of Aleister Crowley and the rituals and teachings of the Hermetic Order of the Golden Dawn. We eventually met in the late 1970s and became friends.

practitioner. After reading it through several times, I knew exactly where I needed to begin.

Regardie suggests that planetary talismans[5] can be helpful in overcoming unfavorable aspects that might be afflicting one's astrological chart. That really drew my attention. I knew I had difficult aspects in my natal chart, so I contacted my brother, Marc[6] (the astrologer), to see which planet could use a little extra help. "All of them," he coldly informed me. But, because it rules my chart, he suggested I first try to make better friends with the Moon.

With Regardie's little book as my guide, I started gathering symbols for a Lunar talisman on January 23. At midnight on January 27, after anointing it with drops of dew that had formed in the moonlight falling on my 1952 Chrysler, I consecrated it with as much ceremony as I was capable of devising.

My Moon talisman was the most beautiful thing I had ever made with my own two hands. It was a double-circle model made of card stock. I extracted the sigils of the Lunar spirit and intelligence from the moon kamea[7] in the book and carefully drew them in silver paint against a field of deep violet[8] drawing ink on the front and back of one of the circles. On the other circle, I painted a silver

---

5   Sometimes called amulets, talismans are small objects often bearing magical symbols and/or words created with magical intent and charged with a specific spiritual force. Talismans have traditionally been created and carried on one's person in order to ward off evil, attract good luck, or for other magical purpose.

6   Marc E. DuQuette. b. 1942. Author of *Orange Sunshine—How I Almost Survived America's Cultural Revolution* (Los Angeles, CA: Self-published, 2008).

7   A kamea, or normal, magick square consists of the distinct positive integers 1, 2, ... n^2, such that the sum of the n numbers in any horizontal, vertical, or main diagonal line is always the same. A kamea of Luna is a square 9 × 9 (Luna being attributed to the ninth planetary sphere or Sephirah on the Tree of Life). Kameas for the other planets are: Saturn, 3 × 3; Jupiter, 4 × 4; Mars, 5 × 5; Sol, 6 × 6; Venus, 7 × 7; and Mercury, 8 × 8. The Hebrew letter or letters numerically equivalent to the numbers that occupy each kamea's squares can then be used to spell out any word or name.

8   Silver and violet are both colors sacred to the Moon.

image of the elephant-headed Hindu god Ganesha[9] (to whom the Moon is sacred) on one side, and on the other side painted the appropriate planetary and geomantic symbols. Around one perimeter, I wrote in Hebrew the divine and angelic names, and on the reverse side part of the Psalm 72 *"... abundance of peace so long as the moon endureth."* When it was finished, I lovingly slipped it inside a linen bag I had sewn with violet thread. On the flap I embroidered a silver crescent moon.

I was very proud of myself, but I still didn't feel like much of a magician. I did carry it around for a few days and felt curiously empowered—but empowered to do *what,* I didn't know. I wasn't sure what I should do next. The answer came (as so many important answers do) while I was taking a shower. I should make all seven of the planetary talismans!

For the next four months, with the help of Regardie's little book, and using my ever-improving artistic and magical skills, I created and consecrated a full set of seven planetary talismans. Each one was more beautiful and worshipful than its predecessor. The order in which I created them was dictated by the severity of the planetary afflictions in my natal chart. I consecrated the Mars talisman on February 6. By then I had taught myself the Supreme Invoking Ritual of the Pentagram and Hexagram, which from then on became an integral part of my talisman consecration rituals.

Jupiter was next on February 27 (Constance's birthday), followed by Venus exactly one month later. The Venus talisman evoked the most remarkable reactions. My dreams were filled with vividly erotic encounters, the likes of which I had not experienced since adolescence. They continued until April 4, when I consecrated my talisman of Mercury, when my dreams turned anxious and confusing. (Oh well!)

---

9 See chapter 11.

I started the Saturn talisman on May 10 and consecrated it at midnight on the thirteenth. The next day, I started to collect the symbols for my seventh and last planetary talisman. Sol took ten days to complete. I consecrated it during a lunar eclipse[10] that took place on May 24. My arsenal of planetary talismans was finally complete.

Throughout this entire talisman-making period and the months that followed, life at the DuQuette house continued to be a litany of chaos, frustration, and despair. In an attempt to make money doing something other than singing in saloons, I accepted a house-painting job and we moved to the San Gabriel Valley. As it turned out, I would never be paid for my (admittedly inept) labor and we found ourselves stranded in La Verne, the smoggiest town in Southern California, with no job and no money.

July 11 dawned with the prospect of the worst birthday of my life. About 11:15 in the morning, I shut myself in my bedroom temple. I lit a candle and put it on my altar top. I halfheartedly performed the Banishing Rituals of the Pentagram and Hexagram and sat down and tried to meditate. I couldn't. To cheer myself, I removed my cherished talismans from their bags and lingered on every detail of their splendor. As I turned them in my fingers, I whispered the words of power and the names of the gods, angels, and spirits inscribed on each one of them. Finally, as if to bring order to my otherwise unordered universe, I placed the Sun talisman in the center of the altar top and surrounded it with the six remaining planets in their proper hexagram positions.[11] They were so beautiful—so perfect.

---

10 I thought it would be "heavy" and magical to do a magical operation during a lunar eclipse. I later would learn this is usually not the best time to work. Still, I lived through it.

11 Sun in the center, Saturn the top point, Jupiter upper right, Mars upper left, Venus lower right, Mercury lower left, and Luna at the bottom point.

For a moment, I didn't know how to feel. I was alternately depressed and elated; depressed that these talismans were the *only* things perfect in my life, and elated that at least *something* was perfect in my life. I looked at the clock. It was almost noon and time to rejoin Constance and little Jean-Paul for birthday cake. They were both giggling in the kitchen. Their laughter made me giggle too. And then, in a clichéd moment—an epiphany worthy of a Frank Capra film—I realized that there were *lots* of perfect things in my life. In fact, at that moment I was the luckiest man on earth.

My melancholy lifted. I credited the talismans for my change of mood. As I gazed at them there on the altar top, I realized that they would never be more beautiful or meaningful to me than they were at that moment. In just a few weeks, their colors would start to fade, the inks would crack, the edges wear. In a few years, I would probably lose some of them, and those that remained would shrivel into crumbling bits of brittle card stock. I wished I could preserve them forever just like this—at the zenith of their strength—in an eternal environment where their beauty would never be effaced—a place where their power could never diminish.

These talismans were no good to me sitting on my altar top or tucked away in their sterile little bags. I needed them to literally become part of me. No! More than that—I must use their magick to make me *someone else*—someone new. I must reabsorb my precious planetary children and plant them in the womb of my own soul. I must impregnate myself with their magical potency and, by doing so, beget upon myself a *new* self.

One by one, I joyously plunged the seven talismans into the sacred fire of the altar candle flame. I inhaled their light and heat as the frail husks of paper and ink were reduced to a clean white ash.

It was noon, July 11, 1975—the first moment of my life as a magician.

|||||||||||||||||||||||||||||||||||||||||||||||||||||||||||||||||||||||||||||||||||||||||||||||||||||||||||||||||||||||||||||||

SIX

A WEEKEND ALONE WITH THE
SPIRITS OF THE TAROT[1]

You hold the universe in your hand when you pick up a deck of tarot cards.

RABBI LAMED BEN CLIFFORD

The creation and ritual "consummation" of my seven planetary talismans launched me on a wondrous magical adventure that I am only now (at the dawn of my reflective years) beginning to put in perspective. In the years that immediately followed that birthday immolation, I would unexpectedly undergo magical initiation at the hands of some of the last surviving personal students of Aleister Crowley, find myself leading a magical lodge, and become friends with many of the brightest magical minds in the world, including Robert Anton Wilson, Christopher S. Hyatt, and Francis (Israel) Regardie. I would undergo (one might say suffer) an

---

1 I first shared the outline of this ceremony in an address to the 2003 Los Angeles Tarot Symposium, and in the Beltane 2005 issue of *Pentacle Magazine*, UK.

Odyssean array of personal and magical ordeals, challenges, triumphs, and tragedies.

Among the subjects that captured my imagination (and spare time) in the first two decades of my journey was tarot and its relationship (at least in the minds of hermetic magicians) to the Qabalah. I realize that probably not everyone reading this book is familiar with tarot, but it is highly likely that many of you are. Those of you who read the cards for yourself or for others probably have a favorite deck that you've used for a long time—a deck you trust; a deck you've charged with your own personal essence and vibrations; a deck you've empowered through years of repeated use. If you do, it's probably scuffed and dog-eared. Its edges are most likely filthy gray from years of skin-oil and dirt. It just might be a biohazard! I know many tarot readers whose cards are so flaccid they hardly make any noise when they are shuffled.

But, unattractive as your well-worn cards may be, you probably view them as old friends. You have a history together. You trust them. They are alive—perhaps more alive than you can imagine.

My first deck of tarot cards was one I painted myself as part of the marvelous Builders of the Adytum (B.O.T.A.)[2] Tarot/Qabalah correspondence course back in the early 1970s. It was sort of a paint-by-numbers project (only without the numbers), and I had worked on only the twenty-two trumps. I didn't attempt to read or divine with those cards because the lessons cautioned that one could cripple oneself spiritually by using the cards to tell fortunes. I took the warning seriously—for a while.

The deck I first used to read the cards was an early edition of the *Thoth Tarot*[3] deck that I bought in 1972 at Pickwick Bookstore in Costa Mesa. I would use that deck exclusively for more

---

2 Builders of the Adytum (B.O.T.A.) is a religious nonprofit, tax-exempt, California corporation founded by Paul Foster Case (1884–1954).

3 Since the early 1970s, the *Thoth Tarot* has been printed by an assortment of publishers.

than twenty years. I might still be using it but, as fate would have it, I would eventually create my own tarot deck, *The Tarot of Ceremonial Magick*,[4] and I guess I would be a poor advertisement if I didn't use my own deck. I would eventually come to realize that the creation of *The Tarot of Ceremonial Magick* was really a continuation and elaborate expansion of the magical operation that I started years earlier by creating my seven planetary talismans—for indeed, the tarot is one magnificent and complex talisman containing within its matrix all the usual suspects of the Western hermetic and magical traditions. Please don't think that I am suggesting that, in order to successfully use the cards as a divinatory tool, a person has to be aware of all the astrological and magical virtues of the seventy-eight cards. In fact, I'd wager that the majority of tarot readers in the world couldn't care less about the underlying magical principles, forces, and spirits inherent in the cards. Yes. I said *spirits*—but I'll get to that in a moment.

Because it is built upon fundamental Qabalistic principles, tarot is in a very real way the graphic DNA of the hermetic arts that are also Qabalah-based, including astrology, alchemy, and several varieties of ceremonial magick. As such, tarot is (or should be) of special interest to magicians and would-be magicians.

If we could magically peek just below the slick surface and colored inks of tarot cards, we would see that every pack is a tidy little block of flats that houses a teeming world of angels, spirits, and demons. For centuries an odd assortment of obsessed holy guys (who obviously had a lot of time on their hands) identified, fingerprinted, and booked these spirit creatures, and with zealous and anal-retentive attention to detail, categorized them by their elemental, planetary, zodiacal, astrological, and other traditional correspondences.

---

4 Lon and Constance DuQuette, *Tarot of Ceremonial Magick: A Pictorial Syntheses of Three Great Pillars of Magick (Astrology, Enochian Magick, Goetia)*. Originally published by U.S. Games Systems, Inc., 1994. Newest edition by Thelesis Aura, 2010.

Then, with the ruthlessness of tenement landlords, these holy guys squeezed each of them into its appropriate place in the spiritual hierarchy of the cosmos—referenced and cross-referenced in mountains of ancient and modern tables, graphs, and charts. This information has always been implied by the structure of the tarot but, until I designed my deck, this information (or at least the major landmarks of this information) was never overtly displayed on a deck of tarot cards themselves. I wanted to make flash cards of pertinent data relating to Astrology and the two most widely practiced varieties of magick (Enochian[5] and Goetia[6]), and that's just what I did—first in crude, hand-drawn notecards for the edification of my Monday night magick class, then later in the more heroic published deck. A couple of weeks before the first edition of my deck went on sale worldwide, I did the very best I could to magically charge the cards by invoking, evoking, or otherwise magically activating their spirit tenants. If you have a moment, I'd like to tell you how it was done.

The afternoon I opened the UPS package and took out the first box of my tarot cards was one of the most magical moments of my life. The project had taken the better part of five years from design to manifestation. Oh, how I savored the moment! I sat down in my big papa-chair and turned the box over and over in my hands. I closed my eyes and held it up to my nose and inhaled the exotic incense of plastics and inks and resins. I tried to picture in my mind the factory in faraway Belgium where they were printed, cut, and packaged. I tried to imagine how all ten thousand boxes

---

5 Enochian magick is a magical system developed in the late sixteenth century by Dr. John Dee and Edward Kelley. Aspects of the complex system were expanded upon in the late nineteenth century by adepts of the Hermetic Order of the Golden Dawn and later by Aleister Crowley. See my *Enochian Vision Magick—An Introduction and Practical Guide to the Magick of Dr. John Dee and Edward Kelley* (York Beach, ME: Weiser Books, 2008).

6 DuQuette, *Tarot of Ceremonial Magick*.

might look stacked up in a pyramid. For some reason, however, I was hesitant to open that first box and break the clear plastic wrapper that bound the deck into one perfect, *virgin* entity.

"Why can't I open the box?" I asked myself.

Even as I mentally broadcast that question, the answer returned on the same thought-wave.[7]

A deck of tarot cards is a wondrous thing. According to tradition, tarot was designed, organized, and arranged to be a perfect reflection of the cosmic principles that create and sustain all things in heaven and earth.[8] Tarot is a telescope through which we can gaze at the great macrocosmic world of deity; and it's a microscope by which we can dissect the tiniest secrets of nature and our own souls. But, unless we are somehow cognizant of this Qabalistic perfection, either intellectually or intuitively, tarot is just seventy-eight pieces of printed card stock.

Sitting there in my big chair, I was paralyzed with the realization that this was a rare and magical moment. It would be weeks before the cards would be on the market—weeks before other hands would touch them and other eyes behold the images. For this golden moment, the deck I held in my hand was the virgin *mother deck*—the virgin *father deck*—the immaculate *archetype* of all the decks of my *Tarot of Ceremonial Magick* that would ever be printed and sold in the future.

For a magician, this was an once-in-a-lifetime opportunity. I had the chance to charge and attune this mother deck with all the powers and properties that lay hidden in all tarot decks. I had the chance to literally invoke upon (and evoke into) this deck all the spiritual forces, aspects of deity, archangels, angels, intelligences,

---

7 A phenomenon that often characterizes spirit communication. See chapter 13.

8 Whether or not this is a historical fact, the current structure of a standard deck of tarot cards has nevertheless evolved over the centuries to represent a perfect reflection of basic Qabalistic principles.

and spirits that magical tradition informs us are resident in each card.

I had the chance—no—I had the *responsibility* to magically charge this deck as no deck of tarot cards has ever been charged, and, in doing so, transmit that charge to all its cloned children throughout the world!

(Perhaps you are hearing the *"Mwa-ha-ha-ha-ha-hah!"* of mad scientist laughter?)

This obviously would be a big job, requiring many hours, perhaps days, to complete. I would need to draw upon all the knowledge and skill a mad, narcissistic, and obsessed magician (with far too much time on his hands) could muster. Constance was out of town visiting her parents in Nebraska. I had the house all to myself. I had a three-day weekend before me... and of course, most importantly—*I was just the mad, narcissistic, and obsessed magician who could do it!*

I set immediately to work. I unplugged the telephone, then showered and dressed in clean black sweatpants and a white T-shirt. (This wizard needs to be clean and comfortable!) I then cleared the furniture from the center of the living room. "If Constance knew I was doing this she'd kill me! Ah, but she won't know until she gets back from Nebraska. *Mwa-ha-ha-ha-ha-hah!*" For the next two days, this space would be my temple.

I am pretty much a fly-by-the-seat-of-my-pants magician, but there are certain magical formulae that I never fail to acknowledge and incorporate in my operations. The most venerable of these concerns the preparations I make prior to an operation. I had already done the first prerequisite, that of bathing myself and putting on clean clothes. Now it was time to do something similar to the area in which I would work.

I thoroughly vacuumed the living room carpet, then proceeded with the more formal ceremonies. I started by anointing the top of my head with holy oil (Oil of Abramelin[9]), then I *banished* the temple with the standard Banishing Rituals of the Pentagram and Hexagram. These two ceremonies served the purpose of clearing the temple completely of elemental and planetary influences. The room was now, for the moment, a magical vacuum. From that moment on, the only magical forces to enter this sacred space would be those that I specifically allowed in.

Next I *purified* the temple with water. There are many elaborate ceremonies I could have used, but instead I went to the kitchen and grabbed my favorite coffee cup[10] and filled it with tap water. I stuck the forefinger of my right hand in it and stirred it around for a moment. There! I had manufactured my own holy water. (As a duly consecrated bishop,[11] I can do that.) I returned to the living room and sprinkled the floor east, south, west, and north. At each quarter I simply pronounced an impromptu, "I purify the temple with water."

Next I *consecrated* my temple with fire. I took a votive candle off the fireplace mantle and lit it. I approached each quarter of the room as before and drew in the air an equal-armed cross with the flame with the words, "I consecrate the temple with fire and dedicate this space to the purpose of this act of magick."

There. I was almost ready to get to work—but get to work doing what? Standing there in my nice clean body and clothes, in the nice clean empty universe of my living room temple, I needed now to announce to myself and the magical cosmos what exactly I was here for. I had to frame my magical intention in words. I had to take the

---

9 Considered by many magicians to be the most sacred and powerful of magical unguents, Oil of Abramelin was first mentioned in *The Sacred Magic of Abramelin the Mage*, written in 1458 by Abraham the Jew. It is made up primarily of pure cinnamon oil, olive oil, and small amounts of oil of myrrh and galangal.

10 When you think about it, what more personal, practical, and sacred magical vessel is there for a coffee drinker?

11 See chapter 13 and appendix 2.

oath. I grabbed my magical diary and a pen and quickly composed an oath that encapsulated my magical intent for this operation. I fired up some charcoal in the censer and covered it with pure frankincense. As the sweet-smelling smoke rose to the heavens, so did my ninety-three-word oath:

> I, Adeo Sat Bene,[12] Zealator and Ninth Degree, swear to the Supreme *What-It-Is* of the Universe that I will charge this deck of tarot cards and every other deck of this design that currently exists, or will exist in the future, with the force of every spiritual entity in the universe that I am capable of conjuring and binding into it. May their presence in the cards serve to contribute only to the enlightenment and spiritual health and well-being of all with whom it comes in contact. So mote it be!

With the banishing, purification, and oath out of the way, I got down to business. I would start by charging the fifty-six cards of the tarot's Lesser Arcana: The four Aces (Ace of Wands, Ace of Cups, Ace of Swords, Ace of Disks) the sixteen Court Cards (four per suit—a Knight, a Queen, a Prince, a Princess), and thirty-six Small Cards or pips (2 through 10 of each suit).

In the middle of the floor, I assembled several items of the elaborate magical equipment associated with the Enochian magick of Dr. John Dee. For this operation I would use the four *Elemental Tablets* and the small *Tablet of Union* that rules them. These tablets and the way they are constructed have a direct correlation to the structure and organization of the tarot. They offered me the perfect consecrated centerpiece for my operation.

---

12 My magical motto is "Adeo Sat Bene." It is Latin for "So far, so good."

Space does not permit me here[13] to elaborate fully on the magical significance of the Enochian Tablets. But, in order for this part of the story to make any sense at all to anyone who is completely unfamiliar with Enochian magick, I must at least point out a few landmarks of the system—particularly those that modern Enochian magicians refer to as "Elemental Tablets." There are four of them; one each for fire, water, air, and earth. Each Elemental Tablet is made up of 156 squares or truncated pyramids arranged in a large tablet twelve squares wide by thirteen squares high. Each pyramid is lettered with the one-letter-name of an elemental angel. Combined with one, two, or many other letters within the tablet, an almost infinite number of larger and more complex angels are generated, forming an elaborate (and painfully logical) hierarchy of elemental angels. It is a breathtakingly elegant system, and can be the subject of a lifetime of study.

This system parallels the hermetic structure of the tarot. The four Elemental Tablets are the equivalent of the four Aces of the tarot. For example; put the Ace of Wands under a magick microscope and you will see the entire Enochian Elemental Tablet of Fire teeming with the living hierarchy of angels that inhabit it. Do the same with the Ace of Cups and see the Elemental Tablet of Water; the Ace of Swords for the tablet of Air, and the Ace of Disks for the tablet of Earth.

---

13 But I have written a very nice introduction to the subject that I am not shy about urging you to read. *Enochian Vision Magick—An Introduction and Practical Guide to the Magick of Dr. John Dee & Edward Kelley* (York Beach, ME: Weiser Books, 2008).

Each Elemental Tablet is equivalent to a tarot Ace.

Each of the Enochian Elemental Tablets is subdivided into four equal-sized quarters by a cross made up of two vertical columns and one row. This cross is made up of thirty-six lettered squares (more on that in a moment). Each of the four quarters created by this cross is assigned to one of the four elements. For example: the fire tablet has a quarter for fire (fire of fire), one for water (water of fire), one for air (air of fire) and one for earth (earth of fire). The Elemental tablets of water, air, and earth are divided in exactly the same way.

These subquarters (often called subangles) of the four Elemental Tablets are the equivalent to the sixteen Court Cards of the tarot. The Knights are fiery, the Queens watery, the Princes airy, and the Princesses are earthy aspects of their respective suits.[14]

For example: put the Knight of Wands (fire of fire) under a magick microscope and behold the fire quarter of the Elemental Tablet of fire and all the Enochian angels living inside it. Look at the Queen of Disks (water of earth) with the magick microscope and see the water quarter of the Elemental tablet (Ace) of earth, etc. I'm sure you are getting the picture.

---

14 Or in many standard decks, the fire, water, air, and earth Court Cards are King, Queen, Knight, and Page.

Each Elemental Tablet is divided into four sub-elemental quarters which are equivalent to the four tarot Court Cards of each suit.

The remaining cards of the Lesser Arcana are the thirty-six Small Cards (or pips), the 2s through 10s of each of the four suits. The Small Cards also are populated by a rich assortment of traditional spirits, angels, and demons, many of which are arranged in neat hierarchical families dictated by their place in the zodiac and the zodiacal year.

[Warning! If all this technical Enochian magick talk is putting you to sleep—Wake up! It's going to get good!]

Each of the thirty-six Small Cards represents one decan (ten degrees) of the zodiac. In groups of three:

- The nine Small Cards of the suit of Wands naturally live in the three fire signs of the zodiac (Aries, Leo, and Sagittarius).
- The nine Cups live in the water signs (Cancer, Scorpio, Pisces).
- The nine Swords live in the air signs (Libra, Aquarius, Gemini).
- The nine Disks live in the earth signs (Capricorn, Taurus, Virgo).

Starting at 0 degrees Aries, these thirty-six Small Cards spread themselves in perfect 2-3-4-5-6-7-8-9-10, 2-3-4-5-6-7-8-9-10, 2-3-4-5-6-7-8-9-10, 2-3-4-5-6-7-8-9-10, order through the zodiac with elegant simplicity:

- All four groups of 2-3-4s inhabit the *cardinal signs* of the zodiac (Aries, Cancer, Libra, and Capricorn).
- The four sets of 5-6-7s reside in the *fixed signs* of the zodiac (Leo, Scorpio, Aquarius, and Taurus).
- The four sets of 8-9-10s find themselves neatly housed in the *mutable signs* of the zodiac (Sagittarius, Pisces, Gemini, and Virgo).

2 3 4	5 6 7	8 9 10	2 3 4	5 6 7	8 9 10	2 3 4	5 6 7	8 9 10	2 3 4	5 6 7	8 9 10
Wands	Disks	Swords	Cups	Wands	Disks	Swords	Cups	Wands	Disks	Swords	Cups
Aries	Taurus	Gemini	Cancer	Leo	Virgo	Libra	Scorpio	Sagittar.	Capric.	Aquarius	Pisces

From left to right, the 36 Small Cards
distributed through the zodiacal year.

The thirty-six squares of the Great Cross of each Elemental Tablet are equivalent to the thirty-six Small Cards (2–10) or each tarot suit. The 2-3-4s (the cards that represent the 30 degrees of the *cardinal signs* of the zodiac) are always positioned in the left-hand column of the Great Cross; the 5-6-7s (the cards that represent the 30 degrees of the *fixed signs* of the zodiac) are always positioned as the horizontal row of the Great Cross; and the 8-9-10s (the cards that represent the 30 degrees of the *mutable signs* of the zodiac) are always positioned in the right hand column of the Great Cross. The ordering of the cards within their respective columns and row, however, differ between the four Elemental Tablets.

					2	8					
					3	9					
					4	10					
					2	8					
					3	9					
					4	10					
5	6	7	5	6	7	5	6	7	5	6	7
					2	8					
					3	9					
					4	10					
					2	8					
					3	9					
					4	10					

*The 36 squares of the Great Cross of each Enochian Elemental Tablet
are equivalent to the 36 Small Cards of the tarot*

The Tablet of Union is sort of like the master ruler or table of contents for the four Elemental Tablets. It is made up of only twenty lettered squares (five wide by four high), but *oh* what squares they are, for those twenty squares contain the entire elemental enchilada.

	SPIRIT Ace	AIR Prince	WATER Queens	EARTH Princess	FIRE Knight
AIR Swords	E	X	A	R	P
WATER Cups	H	C	O	M	A
EARTH Disks	N	A	N	T	A
FIRE Wands	B	I	T	O	M

Tablet of Union

Now that you have had a basic introduction the Enochian way of looking at the elemental world, you'll understand a bit more of the method to the magical madness I was about to embark upon.

I laid the unopened deck of cards upon the Tablet of Union like it was a tiny little virgin on a sacrificial altar and performed a brief baptism ceremony whereby I officially named the deck *Tarot of Ceremonial Magick*. I opened the box and slid out the little white book and the sealed deck. With my thumbnail, I broke the clear plastic hymen and took out the cards. They smelled wonderful! I separated the twenty-two trumps (greater arcana[15]) from the fifty-six cards of the lesser arcana.[16] I would start by charging the lesser arcana.

I placed each Ace in the center of its natural tablet (the Ace of Wands on the Fire tablet, the Ace of Cups on the Water tablet, the Ace of Swords on the Air tablet, the Ace of Disks on the Earth tablet). These lettered tablets, which contain the names of literally thousands of Enochian elemental angels and spirits, are reproduced on the Aces of my deck.

I then placed the sixteen Court Cards upon the appropriate subangles of the four Elemental Tablets. These lettered subangles with their specific hierarchy of spirits are also reproduced in colorful detail on the Court Cards of the deck.

Finally, I arranged the thirty-six Small Cards (nine per tablet) on their appropriate squares of the Grand Cross area of each tablet.

---

15 The twenty-two cards of the *greater arcana* are associated with the twenty-two letters of the Hebrew alphabet, and are often referred to as the "Trumps." They are the cards most people think of when they hear the term "tarot cards." In the *Tarot of Ceremonial Magick* they are numbered 0–21 in the following order: Fool, Magus, High Priestess, Empress, Emperor, Hierophant, Lovers, Chariot, Adjustment, Hermit, Fortune, Lust, Hanged Man, Death, Art, Devil, Tower, Star, Moon, Sun, Aeon, Universe.

16 The fifty-six cards of the *lesser arcana* are divided into the four elemental suits: Wands/Fire; Cups/Water; Swords/Air; Disks/Earth. The Ace of each suit is, as it were, the master card of the suit; the four Court Cards (Knight, Queen, Prince, and Princess) and nine Small Cards (2–10) all "living" inside the Ace. A complete pack of tarot cards contains: Twenty-two trumps; four Aces; sixteen Court Cards; and thirty-six Small Cards.

These individual squares are also reproduced on the Small Cards of the deck.

I opened the temple with the traditional four-part *Opening by Watchtower* ceremony that was used by the Golden Dawn, and then systematically activated the tablets by invoking the *Three Great Secret Names of God* and the seven planetary *Seniors* of each tablet. Then I intoned, in turn, the first eighteen *Calls* in the Enochian angelic language. Over the years I had intoned the Calls many times, but never all at once. It felt very strange, and put me in an altered state of consciousness that intensified as the two-day-and-night ritual would proceed.

It was midnight by the time I was through activating the tablets. I went to bed without banishing in order to let the fifty-six cards of the lesser arcana "fry" all night upon the fully activated Enochian Tablets. In the morning (Saturday), before getting back to magick, I outlined the rest of the marathon ceremony in my journal. There was still a lot of Enochian work ahead of me. For each of the sixteen Court Cards, I had to call upon the three major angels (two *God Names* and *Kerub* of the Calvary Crosses) and four minor angels (the four *servitors* of each subangle). As the tablets were already activated from the night before, this took less than ninety minutes.

After that, the ceremonies turned classically Qabalistic. I called into the thirty-six Small Cards (the 2s–10s of each suit) the seventy-two Angels of the Shemhamphorash, whose names appear on the cards. This took more time than I imagined. I had to first lay out the cards, then intone, in order, each angel name and recite the Psalm that tradition holds is expressive of the duties assigned to each particular angel. (Oh those Qabalists do love their Psalms!)

Next, I turned my attention to evoking into the cards the seventy-two spirits of the Goetia whose names and sigils appear in pairs on each of the thirty-six Small Cards. The spirits of the Goetia are

The spirits of the tarot

Days of the year	Zodiac Sign	Archangel	Angel	Lord by Day	Lord by Night	Angel of the Decans	Decan	72 Angels of the Shem ha-Mephorash	Tarot Suit	Tarot Small Card	Title of Small Card	Day / Night Demon (72 Demons of the Goetia)	Qliphotic Genius	Order of the Qliphoth
JUNE Jun 21 – Jul 1	CANCER Cardinal Water	Muriel	Pakiel	Raadar	Akel	Mathravash	0°-10°	Eiael / Habuiah	CUPS	2	LOVE	BUER (Day) / BIFRONS (Night)	Characith	SHICHIRIRON Black Ones
JULY Jul 2-11						Rahadetz	10°-20°	Rochel / Ilbamiah		3	ABUNDANCE	GUSION (Day) / VUAL (Night)		
Jul 12-21						Alinkir	20°-30°	Haiaiel / Mumiah		4	BLENDED PLEASURE	SITRI (Day) / HAAGENTI (Night)		
Jul 22 – Aug 1	LEO Fixed Fire	Verkiel	Sharaiel	Sanahem	Zaibarheth	Losanahar	0°-10°	Vehuiah / Ieliel	WANDS	5	STRIFE	BELETH (Day) / CROCELL (Night)	Temphioth	SHALHEBIRON Flaming Ones
AUGUST Aug 2-11						Zachi	10°-20°	Sitael / Elemiah		6	VICTORY	LERAIE (Day) / FURCAS (Night)		
Aug 12-22						Sahiber	20°-30°	Mahashiah / Lelahel		7	VALOUR	ELIGOS (Day) / BALAM (Night)		
Aug 23 – Sep 1	VIRGO Mutable Earth	Hamaliel	Shelathiel	Laslara	Sasia	Ananaurah	0°-10°	Aehaiah / Cahethel	DISKS	8	PRUDENCE	ZEPAR (Day) / ALLOCES (Night)	Yamatu	TZAPHIRIRON Scratchers
SEPTEMBER Sep 2-11						Rayadyah	10°-20°	Haziel / Aladiah		9	MATERIAL GAIN	BOTIS (Day) / CAMIO (Night)		
Sep 12-22						Mishpar	20°-30°	Lauiah / Hahiah		10	WEALTH	BATHIN (Day) / MURMUR (Night)		
Sep 23 – Oct 2	LIBRA Cardinal Air	Zuriel	Chedeqiel	Thergebon	Achodraon	Tarasni	0°-10°	Ieiazel / Mebahel	SWORDS	2	PEACE RESTORED	SALLOS (Day) / OROBAS (Night)	Lafcursiax	ABIRIRON Clayish Ones
OCTOBER Oct 3-12						Sahamatz	10°-20°	Hariel / Hakamiah		3	SORROW	PURSON (Day) / GREMORY (Night)		
Oct 13-22						Shachdar	20°-30°	Leviah / Caliel		4	REST FROM STRIFE	MARAX (Day) / OSÉ (Night)		
Oct 23 – Nov 1	SCORPIO Fixed Water	Barkiel	Saitzel	Bethchon	Saihaqniab	Kamotz	0°-10°	Leuuiah / Pahliah	CUPS	5	LOSS IN PLEASURE	IPOS (Day) / AMY (Night)	Niantiel	NECHESHTHIRON Brazen Ones
NOVEMBER Nov 2-11						Nundohar	10°-20°	Nelchael / Ieiaiel		6	PLEASURE	AIM (Day) / ORIAS (Night)		
Nov 12-22						Uthrodiel	20°-30°	Melahel / Hahuiah		7	ILLUSIONARY SUCCESS	NABERIUS (Day) / VAPULA (Night)		
Nov 23 – Dec 2	SAGITTARIUS Mutable Fire	Advakiel	Ahoz	Lebarmin		Mishrath	0°-10°	Nithhaiah / Haaiah	WANDS	8	SWIFTNESS	GLASYA-LABOLAS (Day) / ZAGAN (Night)	Saksaksalim	NACHASHIRON Snakey Ones
DECEMBER Dec 3-12						Vehrin	10°-20°	Ieathel / Sahiiah		9	GREAT STRENGTH	BUNÉ (Day) / VALAC (Night)		
Dec 13-21						Aboha	20°-30°	Reiiel / Amael		10	OPPRESSION	RONOVÉ (Day) / ANDRAS (Night)		
Dec 22-31	CAPRICORN Cardinal Earth	Hanael	Samaqiel	Sandali	Aloyar	Misnin	0°-10°	Lecabel / Vasariah	DISKS	2	HARMONIOUS CHANGE	BERITH (Day) / HAURES (Night)	A'ano'nin	DAGDAGIRON Fishy Ones
JANUARY Jan 1-10						Yasyasyah	10°-20°	Iehuiah / Lehahiah		3	MATERIAL WORKS	ASTAROTH (Day) / ANDREALPHUS (Night)		
Jan 10-19						Yasgedibarodiel	20°-30°	Chavakiah / Monadel		4	EARTHLY POWER	FORNEUS (Day) / CIMEIES (Night)		
Jan 20-29	AQUARIUS Fixed Air	Kambriel	Tzakmiqiel	Athor	Polayan	Saspam	0°-10°	Aniel / Haamiah	SWORDS	5	DEFEAT	FORAS (Day) / AMDUSIAS (Night)	Hemethterith	BAHIMIRON Beastial Ones
FEBRUARY Jan 30 – Feb 8						Abdaron	10°-20°	Rehael / Ihiazel		6	EARNED SUCCESS	ASMODAY (Day) / BELIAL (Night)		
Feb 9-18						Gerodiel	20°-30°	Hahahel / Michael		7	UNSTABLE EFFORT	GÄAP (Day) / DECARBIA (Night)		
Feb 19-28	PISCES Mutable Water	Amnitziel	Vakabiel	Ramara	Nathdorlael	Bihelami	0°-10°	Vevaliah / Ielahiah	CUPS	8	ABANDONED SUCCESS	FURFUR (Day) / SEERE (Night)	Qulielfi	NASHIMIRON Malignant Women
MARCH Mar 1-10						Avron	10°-20°	Saliah / Ariel		9	MATERIAL HAPPINESS	MARCHOSIAS (Day) / DANTALION (Night)		
Mar 11-20						Satrip	20°-30°	Asaliah / Mihael		10	PREFECTED SUCCESS	STOLAS (Day) / ANDROMALIUS (Night)		
Mar 21-30	ARIES Cardinal Fire	Malkidiel	Sharhiel	Saterlaton	Saqelavi	Zazer	0°-15°	Vehuel / Daniel	WANDS	2	DOMINION	BAEL (Day) / PHENEX (Night)	Tzuflifu	BEIRIRON The Herd
APRIL Mar 31 – Apr 10						Behahemi	10°-20°	Heahaziah / Amamiah		3	ESTABLISHED STRENGTH	AGARES (Day) / HALPHAS (Night)		
Apr 11-20						Satander	20°-30°	Nanael / Nithael		4	PERFECTED WORK	VASSAGO (Day) / MALPHAS (Night)		
Apr 21-30	TAURUS Fixed Earth	Asmodel	Araziel	Raydel	Totath	Kedamidi	0°-15°	Mebahiah / Poiel	DISKS	5	MATERIAL TROUBLE	SAMIGINA (Day) / RÄUM (Night)	Uriens	ADIMIRON Bloody Ones
MAY May 1-10						Minacharai	10°-20°	Nemamiah / Ieilael		6	MATERIAL SUCCESS	MARBAS (Day) / FOCALOR (Night)		
May 11-20						Yakasaganotz	20°-30°	Harahel / Mizrael		7	SUCCESS UNFULFILLED	VALEFOR (Day) / VEPAR (Night)		
May 21-31	GEMINI Mutable Air	Ambriel	Sarayel	Saraish	Ogarman	Sagarash	0°-10°	Umabel / Iahhel	SWORDS	8	SHORTENED FORCE	AMON (Day) / SABNOCK (Night)	Zamradiel	TZELILIMIRON Clangers
JUNE Jun 1-10						Shehadani	10°-20°	Annauel / Mekekiel		9	DESPAIR & CRUELTY	BARBATOS (Day) / SHAX (Night)		
Jun 11-20						Bethon	20°-30°	Damabiah / Meniel		10	RUIN	PAIMON (Day) / VINÉ (Night)		

traditionally categorized as fallen angels and can be a pretty rough bunch. It's not that they're evil *per se*—just blind, unbalanced forces that do the heavy lifting in the universe. Like heavy machinery, they can be dangerous to the untrained operator, and very helpful to the experienced (or lucky). These critters are divided into thirty-six day spirits and thirty-six night spirits, so naturally, I would have to evoke thirty-six in the daytime and thirty-six at night.

It was nearly noon on Saturday when I started the evocation of the day spirits. I first cast the circle and triangle that would be necessary for that kind of operation. As each of the thirty-six Small Cards plays host to one day spirit and one night spirit, I spread all thirty-six cards in the Triangle together (a tight fit) and evoked, charged, and dismissed the thirty-six day spirits in turn without having to leave the circle. My charge was the same for each spirit: "You will be helpful, obedient, and protective to me and everyone who uses this card and its replicas."

Even with this highly abbreviated procedure, it took nearly four hours. I broke twice for coffee and bathroom breaks and finished with the evocation of the day spirits just before sunset.

I found ripe avocados, corn chips, and cheese in the house, so I made a demonically huge mess in the kitchen then gorged on nachos and guacamole (the fast-food favorite of California magicians whose wives are out of town). Sated, and a little sick to my stomach, I turned on a tape of Respighi's *Pines of Rome* and took a long early-evening nap.

I got up and showered about 11:00 p.m. and repeated the procedure for the thirty-six night spirits. I finished about four o'clock Sunday morning. By then I was in such a state of wild-eyed exaltation and exhaustion that those last thirty-six spirits were the most polite and cooperative beasties I have ever conjured. Still, I barely had enough energy to put the cards back in their box and banish the temple before I crashed.

After a crazy night of the most bizarre and amusing dreams, I lounged around late Sunday morning, then drove to the deli and treated myself to a fresh onion bagel before forcing myself back to work. I was getting really tired of doing magick.

The twenty-two Trumps would be the last cards to get the full treatment. I sat on the living room floor with Aleister Crowley's *777*[17] and a chart listing the traditional archangels, angels, and qliphotic demons of the signs of the zodiac, and surrounded myself in a magical circle made entirely of tarot cards. I placed the three elemental Trumps (*Fool, Hanged Man,* and *Aeon*) nearest me in the center. Around these, I placed the seven planetary Trumps (*Magus, Priestess, Empress, Fortune, Tower, Sun,* and *Universe*). Circling the planets I spread out the twelve zodiacal trumps (*Emperor, Hierophant, Lovers, Lust, Hermit, Justice, Death, Art, Devil, Star,* and *Moon*) all in a great circle surrounding me and the other Trumps.

Around that circle I laid out the thirty-six Small Cards in a huge circle that required me to move some more furniture just to fit it on the floor. Each of the Small Cards represents 10 degrees of the zodiacal year, so I placed them in order starting with the 2 of Wands (0 to 10 degrees Aries) in the nine o'clock position and moving counterclockwise, finally ending with the 10 of Cups (20 to 30 degrees Pisces).

Finally, I positioned the Aces and Court Cards outside the great outer circle according to the quarters they rule. Then I carefully tiptoed into the very center of my tarot mandala and began my final magical chore.

Using the tables from *777*, I lumbered through my butchered Hebrew pronunciation of the appropriate divine names, archangels, angels, spirits, and intelligences for each element, planet, and zodiac sign. It was really... *really* boring!—so boring that it actu-

---

17 Aleister Crowley, *777 and Other Qabalistic Writings of Aleister Crowley,* revised edition (York Beach, ME: Red Wheel/Weiser Books., 1986).

ally induced a state of consciousness that I can only describe as a dull rhythmic electric ecstasy. (Could fatigue and boredom actually be the key to Qabalistic illumination? Constance certainly thinks so!)

When I was done, I just sat there and buzzed like I've never buzzed before. And so did the cards. I was physically drained, emotionally gratified, psychically raw, and more than a bit insane. Even though I was completely sick of performing magick, I had an epiphany concerning the nature of magick—the realization that the only thing a magician can effect change upon is the *magician.* Yes, the cards got charged—but not because I charged them but because I charged *myself* with that crazy two-day ritual.

By five o'clock Sunday afternoon, nearly forty-eight hours after I began, it was over. With tingling fingers I reordered the cards, gave them a big kiss (at the time, I still wasn't sure where my lips ended and the rest of the universe began), and returned the charged cards to their box. I mustered the energy to banish the temple with the Greater Rituals of the Pentagram and Hexagram, and then moved the furniture back into place. I took a long shower and dressed. I rewarded myself with a trip to my favorite Mexican restaurant where I ordered nearly everything on the menu and got good and drunk.

So there it is. You'd be right to point out that it seems like a damned silly thing for a grown man to do with his weekend alone, and perhaps you would be right.

Am I happy with the way it worked? Well...yes. Of course I am. The cards have gotten great reviews and magicians and tarotists all around the world have told me wonderful and magical things they've done with the cards (and wonderful and magical things the cards have done to them). That's exactly what I wanted to happen.

After fifteen years, two printings, and twenty thousand decks sold worldwide, I've recently changed publishers and it looks like the deck will be around for a long time. I have to confess, however, that I wish I had done one more little thing during my forty-eight hours of magical madness. I wish I'd done some magick to make the damned things *sell* better.

‖‖‖

SEVEN

A MIDSUMMER NIGHT'S CURSE

Lord, what fools these mortals be!

SHAKESPEARE[1]

Curses. Now here's a subject for a discussion of low magick!

Do curses work? Have you ever been cursed? I mean really cursed—cursed by someone who believes they know what they're doing and makes no secret of the fact that they've put a curse on you; someone who stands ready to delight in news of your misery and adversities and hungrily take upon themselves karmic responsibility for your every misfortune? Even if you do not believe in the power of curses, it's very unsettling to think that someone out there fears or despises you so much they profess to willfully project a current of malice toward you in a poisonous ray of concentrated hate.

---

1 Puck. *A Midsummer Night's Dream.* Act II, Scene II.

That's why, in a way, it doesn't matter whether you're a believer in curses or not. If somebody has cursed you and you learn about it, *and you feel uncomfortable about it*, then the curse is at least already partially working. How would you handle something like that? How would you go about neutralizing a curse without being dragged deeper into the mad, toxic world of the curser?

This is a story of a misunderstanding, a curse, and an improvised magical operation designed to neutralize the curse. The misunderstanding was between two very dear friends of our family, both of whom are/were practicing magicians. One is a prominent foreign filmmaker (I'll call him F.F.); the other, at the time, a struggling artist and writer (whom I'll call S.A.). One is still living; the other is now sadly deceased. To respect the privacy and memories of both living and dead, I will not reveal their identities other than to say it is likely that both their names would be recognizable to at least a few of you who are reading these words.

S.A. was a huge fan of the work of F.F., and in the autumn of 1981 he convinced me and several other adventurous lodge brothers to travel to upstate New York to attend a film festival where F.F. was to speak and exhibit several of his films. After the event, S.A. and I had an opportunity to have drinks with F.F. and talk at some length. All three of us were students of magick in general, and the magick of Aleister Crowley in particular, so we hit it off like kindred souls. Before we parted, I gave F.F. my phone number and encouraged him to call me the next time he was in the Los Angeles area, adding that he was more than welcome to stay with the DuQuettes while he was in the neighborhood. I never dreamed he would take me up on the offer.

About a week later, I received a call from F.F., who said he was still in the country and staying with a friend in San Diego. He told me that in two days he was scheduled to visit Catalina Island, but, if my offer of hospitality was still open, he would be happy to come stay with us until then. He even offered to bring a copy of his newest film and screen it at our home for our lodge members. It was an outrageously kind and thoughtful offer that I immediately accepted.

Naturally, S.A. was beside himself with excitement and was one of the first to arrive for movie night. Another of our lodge members went to the mall and purchased every copy of one of F.F.'s books that the store had in stock. After an exciting night viewing the film, everybody went home with an autographed copy. It was truly a very memorable event. S.A. stayed late chatting with F.F. and, before heading home, offered to chauffeur him to the Catalina ferry the next afternoon. F.F. accepted.

We were all in bliss over this brief but pleasant brush with celebrity, and I'm happy to say that F.F. continues to this day to be a dear friend to the DuQuette family. Sadly, his friendship with S.A. would not so long endure.

I feel the need to pause and remind the reader that artists of great genius often possess highly mercurial temperaments. They can be high-strung, unpredictable, and moody. Also, at times the creative energy bubbling inside them cannot be contained within the narrow confines of their artistic medium. Occasionally it just bursts out upon the world—sometimes visiting chaotic and devastating effects upon unsuspecting people around them.

A couple of days after dropping F.F. off at the ferry, S.A. received in the mail an elegantly adorned letter from F.F. He excitedly opened it, expecting to find a thank you note or some other such pleasantry F.F. is known for. Instead, he was stunned to find an eloquently composed poem (penned in fine calligraphy) casting a hideous curse upon him. The reason?

It seems that when F.F. arrived at the hotel in Catalina and unpacked his bags, he discovered that a medicine bottle that should have contained doctor-prescribed tablets important to his health and peace of mind had been emptied of its contents and refilled with ordinary aspirin. Understandably upset, yet completely ignoring the possibility of any other explanation, F.F. became convinced that our dear S.A. was the culprit, and that such larceny must be answered with a magical curse.

Naturally, we were all very shocked and confused by the news. As his host, I felt particularly responsible for anything that might have taken place in my home under my watch. I immediately sent F.F. a check to cover what I estimated would cover the cost of refilling his prescription, along with a note affirming my conviction that S.A. would be the last person on earth who would tamper with his luggage or have any interest in that particular medication, and that I was sure there must be some other explanation. F.F. accepted the check and graciously assured me that he did not in any way blame me. However, he held firm in his belief that S.A. was the culprit and that was that.

S.A., of course, was heartbroken. Later, his sadness turned to anger at being accused of such a thing, especially by someone he idolized and only wished would think well of him. In the days that followed, he fell into a dark depression. Even though he'd done nothing wrong, his resentment and frustration had the effect of the curse actually working on him. He performed the standard banishing rituals and took the usual steps recommended for psychic self-defense, but nothing lifted his spirits. I eventually suggested we try something altogether different to neutralize the curse and help our brother snap out of it.

It was my firm belief that this whole matter could be blamed upon a "demon"—not a demon from the *Goetia* or the *Book of Abramelin*—but a *spirit of misunderstanding*. F.F. was simply not seeing clearly—as if his eyes (in a metaphorical sense) had been bewitched. The magical solution became obvious when I took another look at the stationery upon which the curse had been written.

But before I go into that, and so the details of our little curse-breaking ceremony might make more sense to you, I need to share a little more information about the extraordinary life and magical world of F.F., whose connection to the film industry goes back to the early days of sound pictures. In fact, as a young man he appeared in the cast of Max Reinhardt's 1935 masterpiece, *A Midsummer Night's Dream*,[2] the first sound movie of a Shakespeare play ever produced. His participation in this classic production ignited his brilliant imagination and engendered in his young heart a passionate love and fascination for both the art of cinema and themes of magick. The world of *A Midsummer Night's Dream* became an abiding magical reality for him, and he would throughout his life personally identify with its magick. Even the curse he cast upon poor S.A. was written on personalized stationery that was festooned with beautiful and whimsical images of the fairies from *A Midsummer Night's Dream*. The largest image on the parchment sheet was that of Puck, the mischievous aide to Oberon, the king of fairies.

I saw certain haunting parallels between the plot of the play and the events surrounding the misunderstanding that led to the curse. In the play, Oberon wishes to play a trick on Titania, his fairy queen. While she sleeps, he squeezes the juice of a certain plant in her eyes, bewitching her to fall in love with the first creature she gazes on when she awakens. When she does wake up, she casts her eyes upon Bottom, one of the clowns of the play whose head (because of other magical shenanigans) has been magically replaced by that of a donkey. She immediately falls helplessly in love with this monster, which leads to all manner of fun. Confusing matters even further, Puck applies the magick flower juice to the eyes of other characters in the play while they sleep, and *they*

---

2 *A Midsummer Night's Dream*, Warner Brothers, 1935. Directed by William Dieterle and Max Reinhardt (who also produced).

too awake to mistakenly see things incorrectly. Things become hilariously chaotic as misunderstanding piles upon misunderstanding until finally Oberon and Puck apply an antidote (the juice of *another* kind of plant) to the eyes of the bewitched characters, and everything is set right in the end.

Everyone in our family's circle of friends during those years was very familiar with this delightful play. Each summer for many years running, the DuQuettes hosted a backyard *A Midsummer's Night's Dream* party. We would meet early in the evening, divvy up roles, hand out scripts and flashlights, and then, in the company of dear friends and underneath a bright moon and summer stars, we'd sip wine and read through the entire play.[3]

In an ironically adverse way, the similarities between the play and S.A.'s curse were unmistakable. *Something*—some force or circumstance or delusion or bias—had bewitched F.F.'s eyes so that when he discovered his property missing, he blamed the first person who came to his mind—the last person he saw before stepping on to the Catalina ferry—S.A. If only we could apply Oberon's antidote to F.F.'s eyes! We certainly couldn't do it physically, but perhaps there was a way we could do it magically, and so the play itself became the blueprint of a ritual to lift the curse.

Shakespeare was well aware of the mythological and magical properties of plants and herbs. He mentions by name at least eighty varieties in his plays and poems, twenty-six in *A Midsummer Night's Dream* alone! I wanted first to confirm exactly what flower was used by Oberon to bewitch the eyes of Titania and the others, and then, what other flower was used to lift the curse and allow everyone to see things clearly again.

---

3 When he was very young, our son Jean-Paul played the parts of all the minor fairies. As he grew older, he moved to more manly roles. It remains a warm and magical memory for all of us.

In Act II, Scene I, Oberon himself tells us about the first flower when he informs his servant, Puck, precisely what it is, why it is magical, and where he can find it.

> *Oberon.* My gentle Puck, come hither. Thou rememberest
>   Since once I sat upon a promontory,
>   And heard a mermaid on a dolphin's back
>   Uttering such dulcet and harmonious breath
>   That the rude sea grew civil at her song
>   And certain stars shot madly from their spheres,
>   To hear the sea-maid's music.
>
> *Puck.* I remember.
>
> *Oberon.* That very time I saw, but thou couldst not,
>   Flying between the cold moon and the earth,
>   Cupid all arm'd: a certain aim he took
>   At a fair vestal throned by the west,
>   And loosed his love-shaft smartly from his bow,
>   As it should pierce a hundred thousand hearts;
>   But I might see young Cupid's fiery shaft
>   Quench'd in the chaste beams of the watery moon,
>   And the imperial votaress passed on,
>   In maiden meditation, fancy-free.
>   Yet mark'd I where the bolt of Cupid fell:
>
>   <u>It fell upon a little western flower,</u>
>   <u>Before milk-white, now purple with love's wound,</u>
>   <u>And maidens call it **love-in-idleness**.</u>[4]
>
>   Fetch me that flower; the herb I shew'd thee once:
>   The juice of it on sleeping eye-lids laid
>   Will make man or woman madly dote
>   Upon the next live creature that it sees.
>   Fetch me this herb; and be thou here again
>   Ere the leviathan can swim a league.

---

4 Bold type and underlines my own.

In Shakespeare's day, love-in-idleness was the name of a violet and white European wildflower, also called heartsease (*Viola tricolor*), which was the ancient ancestor of the pansy. His description of the mythical genesis of the flower (that of being created when Cupid's arrow missed the heart of "*a fair vestal throned by the west*") is a not-so-subtle reference to Queen Elizabeth I, whose virgin heart was officially never pierced by Cupid's arrow. The purple of "*love's wound*" of the once-pure-white flower was a poignant reference to the fact that Elizabeth had shunned the personal pleasures of marriage, and the garment that would have been her white bridal dress was transformed by greater duty to the royal purple of the monarchy. She quite literally became the bride of England.

When you think about it, there was big magick in that flower. The sexual power of Cupid's arrow, shot "*as it should pierce a hundred thousand hearts,*" instead of casting a powerful spell of passion on the great queen, injected all its love magick into that tiny quivering flower. I love this stuff!

The identity of the other flower (the one Oberon used to free Titania and the others from the spell of misunderstanding) can be found in Act IV, Scene I:

> *Oberon.* But first I will release the fairy queen.
> Be as thou wast wont to be;
> [*Touching her eyes with an herb*]
> See as thou wast wont to see:
> **Dian's bud o'er Cupid's flower**
> Hath such force and blessed power.
> Now, my Titania; wake you, my sweet queen.

Dian's bud (*Artemisia absinthium*) is named for the chaste goddess of the hunt (another virgin). It is the archaic name for absinthe or wormwood. Associated with sorcery from prehistoric times, its feathery, greenish-gray leaves are poisonous in concentrated doses and produce a narcotic effect in smaller doses. This was starting to sound like serious pharmacology.

The basic format of our ritual was to be very simple. After due preparation, we would have S.A. smear certain parts of the curse parchment with the juice of a love-in-idleness plant. These parts would include F.F.'s signature, the image of the mischievous Puck, and particular words and phrases that most demonstrated F.F.'s temporary inability to see things accurately.

Then, once the curse itself was anointed and fully "alive" with the delusional "spirit" of misunderstanding, S.A. would neutralize the spirit by liberally smearing the juice of Dian's bud upon those same areas of the parchment. All of this, of course, would be accompanied by appropriate incantations gleaned from the works of Shakespeare. The whole operation promised to be not only magically viable, but also a lot of fun.

We chose for our magical temple one of the most beautiful places on earth—the Huntington Library and Botanical Gardens in San Marino, California. Nestled within its 140 acres is a charming Shakespeare Garden containing many of the herbs and plants mentioned in Shakespeare's works—all with little plaques displaying the names of the plays in which they made their appearance. It would be no trouble at all to find our Love-in-idleness and Dian's bud, but how would we pluck them up without drawing the attention of the groundskeepers? *"Ay, there's the rub."*

It was a cool Sunday afternoon when Constance and I, S.A., and a handful of interested lodge members carpooled up to the Huntington. As expected, the place was crowded. The Shakespeare Garden, however, was nearly deserted and it took us no time at all to locate and feloniously pluck up a pocketful of each of our flowers. Before leaving the Shakespeare Garden for more private environs on the grounds, we placed a small offering of some of our ill-gotten herbs at the stone bust of Shakespeare to invoke the presence and blessing of the immortal Bard. After all, he would play the deity role in this magical drama.

The spirit Ariel's greeting to the magician, Prospero, from *The Tempest* served as our invocation:

> All hail, grave master! I come
> To answer thy best pleasure; be't to fly,
> To swim, to dive into the fire, to ride
> On the curled clouds...[5]

We then strolled down to the lily ponds and found ourselves a quiet spot in the shade of a giant magnolia tree and set to work. We all sat on the ground and surrounded S.A. to shield his magical operation from prying eyes. The ceremony was short and very simple. S.A. crushed the love-in-idleness between his hands and rolled them back and forth until the plant was pulpy and wet. He then smeared the areas of the curse I described above. He then held the anointed paper in his hand while he read Oberon's original "curse." The words didn't exactly match our situation, but we thought they'd do.

> What thou seest when thou dost wake,
> Do it for thy true-love take,
> Love and languish for his sake:
> Be it ounce, or cat, or bear,
> Pard, or boar with bristled hair,
> In thy eye that shall appear
> When thou wakest, it is thy dear:
> Wake when some vile thing is near.[6]

---

5 *The Tempest*, Act I, Scene II.
6 *A Midsummer Night's Dream*, Act II, Scene I.

Then, doing the same with the Dian's bud, he smeared the paper with the antidote, saying;

> Then crush this herb into (F.F.'s) eye;
> Whose liquor hath this virtuous property,
> To take from thence all error with his might,
> And make his eyeballs roll with wonted sight.
> When they next wake, all this derision
> Shall seem a dream and fruitless vision ...[7]

That was it. I banished the "temple" with Puck's closing line:

> If we shadows have offended,
> Think but this, and all is mended,
> That you have but slumber'd here
> While these visions did appear.
> And this weak and idle theme,
> No more yielding but a dream,
> Gentles, do not reprehend:
> if you pardon, we will mend:
> And, as I am an honest Puck,
> If we have unearned luck
> Now to 'scape the serpent's tongue,
> We will make amends ere long;
> Else the Puck a liar call;
> So, good night unto you all.
> Give me your hands, if we be friends,
> And Robin shall restore amends.[8]

We spent the rest of the afternoon enjoying the gardens and art museum. S.A. said he felt much better. We debated whether or not to burn the curse letter. S.A. would have none of it, insisting that

---

7 *A Midsummer Night's Dream*, Act II, Scene II.

8 *A Midsummer Night's Dream*, Act V, Scene I.

he'd like to keep it as a memento. We would later discover that over the years F.F. made something of a habit of cursing people whom he thought had somehow wronged him, and that most of them took it in good humor; some were even amused and flattered at the distinction.

Did our Midsummer Night's Dream ritual work? I guess it's a matter of opinion. S.A. certainly stopped worrying about the curse, and in the years to follow went on to become a successful illustrator and author. His untimely death twenty-six years later was not likely the result of any curses other than those his life choices sadly loosed upon himself.

And F.F.? We would learn from a third party (nearly ten years later) that his friend in San Diego (the one with whom he had stayed in the days just prior to his visit with us) had eventually confessed to the pill substitution, stating it was a foolish act of misguided concern for F.F.'s health and well-being.

And so ends the story of A Midsummer Night's Curse. I hope it has served as an illustration of how magick ceremonies can be drawn from virtually any source that inspires the magician, and that it isn't always necessary to lift a magical ritual directly from the works of John Dee, or the Golden Dawn, or Aleister Crowley, or Gerald Gardner in order to assure that … *Jack shall have Jill; Nought shall go ill; The man shall have his mare again, and all shall be well.*[9]

---

9 *A Midsummer Night's Dream*, Act III, Scene II.

||||||||||||||||||||||||||||||||||||||||||||||||||||||||||||||||||||||||||||||||||||||||||||||||||||||||||||||||||||||||||

EIGHT

ASTRAL PROJECTION:
TRAVELING IN THE SPIRIT VISION
(or, Real Magicians Eat Quiche)

I'm either out of my body or out of my mind.

RABBI LAMED BEN CLIFFORD[1]

All my life I've experienced dreams of flying. These are wonderful
and exciting dreams that are remarkably lucid and detailed. I physically feel intense exhilaration and a thrill in the pit of my stomach as I soar through dream skies, diving and turning and banking
just like an airplane. As I move through the air, objects below shift
toward or away from my view in perfect obedience to my speed,
altitude, and the optical laws of natural perspective—just as if I
were looking out the front of an airplane's cockpit. Only there is no

---

1 From the unpublished works of Rabbi Lamed Ben Clifford in the author's private
collection.

cockpit, no airplane, just me flying like Superman with my dream arms pointed forward into space. It's wonderful. I feel so free, so alive—I want it never to stop.

It's likely that you have had the same or similar experiences, or else have had vivid dreams of jumping down from high places (and not getting hurt), or of swimming and breathing under water. Perhaps you wander your house at night, unclear in your mind whether you are dreaming or awake.

If all this sounds familiar, I don't need to tell you that these moments belong to a unique category of dream experience. I believe they are, in fact, not dreams but a natural phenomenon of human consciousness that is often referred to as (for lack of a more accurate term) "astral projection" or "out-of-body experience" (OBE). The term "astral projection" really is a terribly vague and misleading expression for this variety of experience. Astral? What's *that*? Is astral a *what* or is it a *where*? Is my "astral body" my soul? Is it a body at all? Do I project it into space when I "travel" around in it?

We hear the terms "astral body," "astral plane," and "astral world" thrown around in esoteric conversations as if we were talking about conscious ectoplasmic apparitions floating around geographical locations rather than vibratory frequencies of human consciousness (which is precisely what they are). The fact remains, however, that our adventures in these vibratory frequencies of consciousness often feel disturbingly like *we are* conscious ectoplasmic apparitions floating around geographical locations.

Learning to navigate around this strange universe (which other cultures and other spiritual systems might call "the spirit world") is particularly helpful to the magician who understands the importance of being able to think and function in this subtler world— a world that lies just behind and beyond waking consciousness. Indeed, just as the inventor's intangible idea is the foundation for his or her material invention, this *world* forms the foundation of the material plane of existence. In fact, any magical operation that obliges the magician to see with the mind's eye a symbol, a pentagram, a hexagram, a spirit, or an angel, or a demon, or any spiritual life that inhabits and animates *things* deals directly with this so-called astral dimension. Ancient magicians called the ability to view the spirit nature of things "scrying." The adepts of the Golden Dawn called it "traveling in the spirit vision."

Lucid dreaming is another dimension (pardon the play on words) to this mysterious phenomenon of consciousness. The ancient Egyptians took the skill of lucid dreaming pretty seriously. In fact, the ability to consciously gain control of our dream self and the circumstances of our dream environment may very well have been the cornerstone of the science of dying whose master textbook is the *Egyptian Book of the Dead*. Below is a short excerpt from an article I wrote for the October 2004 issue of *Fate Magazine*[2] that attempts to explain the DuQuette field theory on the subject. Please note that the principle for my theory is based upon the now-almost-universally-accepted premise that the function and powers of the *mind* transcend that of the physical *brain*.

The Egyptian Book of the Dead is a magical text supposedly written by the god Thoth himself. It is designed to give the newly deceased man or woman a fighting chance of hanging on to his or her individual consciousness center by projecting it step-by-step through each phase of the death experience to arrive intact at a higher level of existence.

The basic idea is this: If a dying person can keep the mind focused and occupied on a series of particular ideas and images while the physical body dies, the "self" of the individual can separate from the physical body and take up

2 Lon Milo DuQuette, "Terrors of the Threshold: Astral Projection & The Egyptian Book of the Dead," FATE Magazine Vol. 57, No. 10, Issue 654.

residence in the "mind." The preoccupied mind literally becomes an escape pod that will rescue the self from its attachment to the dying body and brain. At each step along the way, the deceased is required to identify with higher and higher aspects of the mind—a process that continues to create new and subtler escape pods that will keep rescuing the self until it is finally delivered safely (and intact) to the realm of the gods.

The Egyptian Book of the Dead ingeniously organizes this journey of ideas and images to match the landscape and nature of each of the progressively higher levels of consciousness and requires the deceased to perfectly memorize and rehearse each leg of the trip prior to dying.

Every level is guarded by a gatekeeper who must be identified by name and forced to allow the deceased to pass. Even the furniture has names that must be carefully memorized and identified with constant chatter—everything that can be done to bolster the deceased's confidence and keep their mind minutely focused on anything but the temptation of allowing oneself to dissolve like the untrained into the sweet oblivion of death.

At this point you might be asking yourself, "All this may have been fine and good for the initiated royalty of ancient Egypt, but what does it mean to me? I'm not going to school to learn how to die." My staid answer to that question would be, "Aren't you?"

The idea that consciousness separates from the body at the time of death is as old as human introspection itself, and it should be clear to anyone who has ever had *dream* experiences like I've described above that consciousness can and does separate from the body in times of sleep, distress, or during other extraordinary circumstances. Furthermore, during such periods of separation, our astral *senses* are attuned to (and perceive) a dramatically different level of reality.

I wish I could say that I am a skilled astral projector. I'm not. Oh, I get out of my body quite often, and when I'm out I'm pretty skilled at controlling my movements and the circumstance of the vision. But only rarely do I consciously initiate the experience. When I do, it is always at that golden moment (at bedtime or nap-time) as my thoughts are just beginning to take on visual dream-forms, but while I am still conscious of the fact that I also have a physical body slumbering on a real bed. This moment is characterized by a strange noise that I seem to hear not with my ears but in the very center of my brain, then an intense feeling of an electrical current passing through my entire body. That "current" is actually the body we might call the astral body, and the fact that I'm feeling it is the signal that my conscious self is about to take residence in it. At that fragile moment of transition, I am nestled uncomfortably within the general vicinity of my physical body. It is at this moment that I can transfer my consciousness from *I'm in my bed body* to *I'm in this buzzing electrical body.* At this point I can get up, wander around the house (which always looks just a little different than my material house), or take a diving leap into the air and fly straight through the ceiling into the glorious sky.

On most occasions, my out-of-body experiences begin without a conscious effort on my part and within the context of a dream-in-progress. I become conscious within the dream state that I am dreaming and already out. I then become consciously aware of my situation and take control from there. I partially achieve this state when I experience magically induced altered states of consciousness, such as when I purposefully induce a trance in order to scry into tarot cards or Enochian magick tablets and squares.

Most of my projections, however, are those in which I find myself accidentally out, wandering only a few yards away from my snoring body, and this is the story of one such adventure. I wish I could tell you there is some kind of great magical lesson to be learned from this tale. Perhaps there is. But mostly I would like simply to illustrate some of the strange and interesting characteristics of these experiences and, in doing so, encourage you to fearlessly start your own program of exploration.

Before I begin, however, I need to share a strange and often terrifying occurrence that often accompanies out-of-body experiences and which (I believe) has since time immemorial been the cause of all manner of religiously motivated nonsense concerning demons, devils, ghosts, vampires, and the torments of hell. We might call this phenomenon the "terror of the threshold." The dynamics of consciousness that explain this phenomenon are, however, anything but terrifying. In fact, I believe when the facts are properly understood, they are very interesting and at times downright funny.

A few moments ago, I described the ancient Egyptian concept of the "self" of the deceased progressively passing from lower to higher levels of consciousness during the death experience, and how at each new level the mind creates an escape pod for the essential "self" of the individual. These temporary shuttlecrafts are also bodies formed from progressively finer and more subtle energy "material." Yogic literature identifies these various bodies as "astral body" or "etheric body" or "causal body" or "mental body" or "emotional body." These subtle bodies do not necessarily need to be created and cast off only by a person who is dying. Indeed, our thoughts, desires, and emotions are constantly in the process of creating and discarding them the over the course of the agonies and ecstasies of this roller-coaster ride we call everyday life.

If you have this concept clearly in mind, I now put to you the idea that all these discarded bodies live on for a time in the same way a decaying corpse and its hair and fingernails, bacteria, DNA, etc., live on in physical bodies buried in your neighborhood cemetery. The only difference being, these astral corpses remain somewhat *animated* for a period of time while the remaining energy still residually resident in their shell completely decays. And like discarded shells or husks, these astral zombies are made of the heaviest stratum—the slowest and lowest frequencies of energy. They sink to the very lowest levels of the sea of consciousness—the area that is very close to the material plane. This is the borderland between dream and waking consciousness. It is quite literally an astral graveyard.

When we are tired and relaxed, we fall fast asleep and ride an express elevator directly to some pretty high levels of consciousness, those whose environs are revealed in the metaphoric imagery as the dream sky into which we blissfully soar. But if something is burdening our minds and forcing us to slowly drag our sorry astral consciousness kicking and screaming out of our physical body and step-by-step up the back stairs of consciousness, then the first place we slog through on our way "up" is the lowest place in *upland*—the graveyard.

The dramatic terrors and ordeals that candidates of ancient mystery schools were required to undergo during their initiation ceremonies illustrated this frightening, yet ultimately harmless, fact of spiritual life. Because this area is so close to the material plane and the solid coordinates of waking space-time consciousness, the "bodies" that populate the cemetery of your threshold are literally those that are hanging around your neighborhood. That is why so many of these bad "dream" experiences seem to include situations dealing with neighborhood "bad people" who, to all dream appearances, are attempting to violate your home or your body or your loved ones. In nine out of ten of my *terror of the threshold* projections, I find myself trying to chase away neighborhood vandals or (get this … and please forgive my politically incorrect subconscious mind) *deranged homeless people* who are attempting to get in my house. But in the metaphoric reality of this plane of consciousness, that is exactly what they are—homeless bodies who are no longer animated by a living self, drifting in obedience to the laws of cosmic osmoses toward a realm (my house) that is inhabited by an abundance of living. These astral zombies mean no harm. They *mean* nothing because there is no "self" inside to provide them with intent. But boy! They scare the living daylights out of you when you stumble into their world.

A moment ago I mentioned that I am not very good at consciously entering into an out-of-body experience. I think I should probably rephrase that to say, "I am not very good at consciously leaving my body unless I've first gorged myself to near unconsciousness on my wife's spinach or broccoli *quiche.*

It is with no small measure of embarrassment that I confess that, even though I came of mystical age in the psychedelic Sixties—even though I have at one time or another in my sixty-two years on this planet experimented with a cornucopia of mind-altering substances—even though I have labored to control my breathing with pranayama, fasted for days on end—even though I've chanted myself to socially acceptable insanity and engaged in magical rituals that I would never dream of describing to your mother—the strongest and most powerful drug I have ever consciously ingested for the purpose of driving myself out of my physical body is Constance's homemade broccoli or spinach quiche.

I must point out that this dish is not necessarily dangerous to anyone possessing a modicum of common sense and self-discipline. It has, however, challenged the resolve of many a strong-willed magician, and unless you have actually inhaled its savory perfume and laid eyes upon its fluffy buxom filling spilling over the thick flaky fringe of rich shortbread crust—unless you've actually slipped a warm forkful of its buttery ambrosia into your watering mouth and felt the living soul of cream and butter and eggs and scallions spiked with nutmeg and a dozen other spices, and Swiss, Parmesan and Cheddar cheeses explode inside your head—then, my friend, you have no right whatsoever to ridicule the weakness of others.

It is a dish to die for. In fact, on one occasion a dear friend of ours actually suffered a massive heart attack within a few hours of his feast of Constance's spinach quiche, an event that required immediate triple bypass surgery and months of recuperation. I'm happy to say he recovered completely and has reassured us on numerous occasions that the experience was worth the memory of the quiche.

Is it any wonder that a weak-willed and insecure glutton such as myself succumbs to the demons of intemperance whenever I'm confronted with an entire spinach or broccoli quiche during a quiet dinner for two in the privacy of my own home?

The particular out-of-body experience I am about to relate took place five years ago following one such quiet dinner. I must hasten to point out that at that time of my life I had been abusing my body with a litany of bad eating and drinking habits ("crimes against wisdom," as the ayurvedic folks would call it) and I had allowed myself to grow to nearly three hundred pounds. It was not good.

I am happy to say that I have since I have lost more than one hundred pounds and am feeling better than I have my entire life. At the time, however, my weight made sleeping quite challenging. It was great for lucid dreaming and astral projection because I was often tossing and turning in that twilight world between waking and sleeping. But it was terribly frightening when I realized that many of my colorful nocturnal adventures were kicked off by the suffocating effects of sleep apnea and that my astral projections could probably be more accurately described as *near-death experiences!* Still, this season of my life was characterized by a rich assortment of out-of-body experiences, and led to my ability to control and direct the circumstances of my dreams and projections.

I wish I could say that Constance was as excited about my astral adventures as I was. But I can't. In fact, they were often rude and terrifying interruptions to her sleep. She usually knows that I am outside of my body before I do, because I almost always roll over on my back and stick my left arm straight up into the air. I have no idea why I do this, but whenever I do it she wakes her up and grumbles to herself, "Oh no! He's out of his body again. I wonder when he's going to make that *noise?*"

The noise that she dreads is a phenomenon that occurs when my astral body tries to speak, or rather, when my physical vocal cords try to vibrate to the speech impulses coming from my astral body. When I open my astral mouth to say something, my physical mouth back in bed makes the most grotesque and hideously frightening noise...

woooooahhhhhhhHHHAAAAeeeeeeeaaaaaAAAAHHHH!

It's not just a whimper either. I let out a monstrous groan as if I were the most tortured soul in the deepest pit of hell. It's very loud. I can hear it myself and often wake up. It is so loud that Constance is sure our next-door neighbors must be terrified by the sound. I feel so embarrassed. I always think, "Why can't I speak? Why am I making these horrible noises?" But instead of shutting up or trying to wake up, I always try again—only louder—

woooooahhhhhhhHHHAAAA-eeeeeeeaaaaaAAAAHHHH!

That's when Constance has had enough and jabs me in the ribs with her elbow and yells in my ear, "You're out of your body again! Wake up and go back to sleep! And put your arm down!"

I don't recall what the occasion was. Perhaps it was a birthday or an anniversary, or just one of those days Constance was careless enough to innocently ask me, "What would you like for dinner tonight, dear?" My answer was of course, "Broccoli quiche! Please!"

And so began a day of heroic kitchen gymnastics that would give birth to the mystic meal. The quiche itself is made in an oversized pastry dish (not a pie plate) that can easily serve a huge slice to six hungry people. It's not a thin little breakfast quiche either. The rich whipped filling fluffs up to nearly four inches. Two of these pieces was entirely too much for one sane person to eat at one sitting. But it was so good that I begged for another. Constance reluctantly agreed and succumbed to the temptation of another slice herself. When we were finished, we had eaten two-thirds of the massive pie. We were gorged and painfully uncomfortable. Constance began to serve her penance by cleaning up the kitchen and attacking the dishes. I moved to the computer and tried unsuccessfully to write. The remaining one-third of the quiche cooled on the kitchen counter.

An hour later we were both still groaning and holding our bloated bellies (of course I had a much bigger burden). The quiche had cooled enough to be wrapped in plastic and put in the refrigerator, which is exactly what Constance was preparing to do when a spirit of gluttony most foul whispered in my ear and counseled me that tomorrow the quiche would not taste nearly as good as is does right now. It would be a waste—a sacrilege—a crime! Sated or not, we should eat the rest of the quiche before going to bed tonight—and that was that!

Constance would have none of it, but she was too tired and full to argue with me. She went off to a hot bath, and I sat in the darkened living room and ate the rest of the broccoli quiche straight out of its baking dish. I went to bed—too full to stay awake—too full to fall asleep. Constance joined me in a few minutes and fell immediately asleep. Our cat Luis snuggled in his usual place, sandwiched tightly between us. In a few minutes, I became too uncomfortable to remain in my physical body. I heard that crazy sound in the center of my head and felt the familiar electrical buzz. Then, without further fanfare, I floated out of my body on a sickening wave of pure butterfat.

I should point out the fact that I did indeed know that I was in a projection. But I was extremely groggy and wanted very much just to fall deeply asleep and make this all stop! It seemed like I was heading toward that blessed realm when I heard a noise outside at the front door. I rolled over to see if I could hear a bit better.

Constance: Oh God! He's rolled over. I hope he doesn't smash the cat.

Luis the cat: Oh God! He's out of his body again. I think he's lying on my back legs.

Yes! It was clear. Somebody was trying to get into the house. I rolled out of bed and quietly crept out into the hallway.

Constance: Well! There goes his arm. He's out of his body. I'll get no sleep tonight!

Luis the cat: If he rolls over any farther, there won't be room for me!

I tiptoed through the living room to the front door. I peered out the window in the door (completely ignoring the fact that *there is no window* in our front door) and saw three or four shadowy figures crouched on the doorstep. Suddenly, I heard a noise behind me in the living room. "One got in!" I thought. I was right.

As I turned around...

Constance: There he goes rocking back and forth.

Luis the cat: Ouch! Damn it! That hurts! Why doesn't he just die and let me sleep!

...I saw a shadow slip inside the large closet that forms the entire south side of our living room. Once inside the closet, the intruder slowly slid the door closed from the inside. It was a very spooky moment.

Completely ignoring the fact that there is *no closet in our living room*, I stood still while I debated with myself about what I should do.

Constance: At least he's stopped rocking. I wonder if he's breathing.

Luis the cat: zzzzzzzzzzzzzz.

It is at this point that I get completely caught up in the action. Part of me knows I'm projecting and/or in a dream, and part of me doesn't. I start to weigh my options as if there were a real intruder in my real house. "I better be careful. Maybe I can somehow trap him in there and call the police. I don't have a gun or a knife or a club… what can I do?"

Then the thought hit me, "I'm huge. I weigh three hundred pounds. I can just fall on this bastard and crush him to a pulp!"

Constance: zzzzzzzzzzzzzz.

Luis the cat: zzzzzzzzzzzzzz.

I march over to the closet door and violently slide it open. Cowering in the dark corner is a slimy lump of blackness that looks very much like the character Smeagol or Gollum from *The Lord of the Rings*. I suddenly feel I have the power to terrorize this creature out of existence—or at least scare it out of my living room. I muster the most hideous face and swell my titanic bulk to monstrous stature. To assure that my voice will billow with the thunder of ten thousand volcanic devils, I suck in an enormous breath of air…

Constance: Oh no! Here it comes…

Luis the cat: God! He's blowing up! Is he trying to crush me to death?

"I'LL CRUSH YOU!" were the words my astral body voice was trying to bellow, but all that could come out of my physical body back in bed was a blood-curdling…

eeuuyyyyiiiiiiiiiieyeeeLLLLLLLL…

*KRUUSHH*HHH*SHHH

UUUUUUUuuuuuUeh!

Luis the cat then knew for sure I was going to crush him to death. He clawed Constance, desperately trying to pull his back legs out from under me, and when he was free his feet did not touch the floor until he was well outside the bedroom.

I had awakened fully and the realization of what just happened struck me as so funny that I began laughing hysterically (Constance says "maniacally"). She told me I scared her to death, but her main concern was that our neighbors must have heard and had the scare of their lives. We were both certain the police were on their way. What would be my defense... quiche intoxication? Astral projection?

You Know You're Out of Your Body...

- When you feel a thrilling tingling sensation in the pit of your stomach, heart, throat, or back of the neck. When you notice this thrill in a dream, it means you have made the identity shift necessary for an OBE. Perhaps this has something to do with our chakras or psychic centers that serve as exits from the body. If you are lucid at this moment, you can fly or do most anything you can imagine. Ironically, the most difficult thing you can do when you find yourself in this wonderful state is to actually think of something fun and productive to do. Plan ahead.

- When forward or upward movement in a dream becomes difficult or impossible to continue. For example: you are walking down a dream sidewalk, walking up stairs, or driving or bicycling down a road and you suddenly find your legs are too heavy to move or the car or bike breaks down. This indicates that you are moving from a lower/slower vibratory level into a higher/more subtle vibratory level, one that your big fat dream vehicles can't enter. If you are lucid at this moment, you can stop walking or riding or driving and *will* yourself to fly forward, leaving your grosser body behind.

- When you experience forward movement that is interrupted by a curve, right/left turns, or spinning. For example: you are preparing to cross the street or move from one side of a room to the opposite side, but change your mind and move 90 degrees either to the left or right. When you step to the right or left, you are stepping out of your body. Or you are driving a dream car or riding a bicycle very fast and suddenly a curve appears that you are certain you will not be able to make. Or you dream that you are spinning or dancing. The corkscrew effect is also a very common prelude to leaving your body.

- When you hear strange noises—bells, rapping, horns, hissing, thunder. Nearly every OBE is accompanied by strange noises that seem to announce the movement from one plane to the next. No matter what kind of noise it is, it always seems to be "heard" with something other than your ears.

- When you encounter Terrors of the Threshold. Encounters with hideous beings occurs most often when, for one reason or another, you skip the dream transition and are roughly thrust from waking consciousness to an OBE. These are seldom pleasant experiences. I encounter these things when I've had too much to eat and try to sleep it off. I roll in and out of uncomfortable consciousness. I actually think I'm getting out up out of bed, but instead I walk right into the lowest region of the astral plane, which, as we have learned, can be a pretty rough neighborhood.

Warning: Don't eat or drink in dreams, especially with dead people! Greek mythology talks of the "Waters of Forgetfulness" that lure the thirsty newly dead, who, once they've had a little sip, fall into a slumber in which all memory of their past life dissolves. This is a very real phenomenon of the astral plane. If you want to remember your experiences, do not eat or drink anything in an OBE. Especially do not eat or drink anything offered you by someone whom you believe to be a person who has passed away... even a friend or loved one. You may be biting off more than you intend to chew.

|||||||||||||||||||||||||||||||||||||||||||||||||||||||||||||||||||||||||||||||||||||||||||||||||||||||||||||

THAT'S NOT WHAT
INVOCATION IS ABOUT

Ax me no questions 'n ah 'll tell y' no lies!

Queenie, *Showboat*[1]

About fifteen years ago, Constance and I were driving to Huntington Beach to attend a group celebration of the *Rite of Mercury*,[2]
when I perceived myself divinely inspired at a stop light. It was as
if the wing-footed messenger of the gods himself had whispered in
my ear, informing me how I could magically manifest in myself the
spirit and presence of the god Mercury upon the entire gathering.

---

1 *Showboat.* Act I, Scene I.

2 The *Rites of Eleusis* are a series of seven ceremonies, each centered on one of the seven
classical planets of antiquity, constructed by Aleister Crowley to be performed in
public. They were first dramatically performed by Crowley, Victor Neuburg (who
danced), and Leila Waddell (who played violin) in October and November 1910 at
Caxton Hall, London. The Equinox I (6). London, Fall 1911. Reprint. (York Beach,
ME: Weiser Books, 1992). Supplement.

"Am I not the god of liars?"[3] I heard him say as the traffic light turned green. "Honor and invoke me tonight by speaking nothing but lies!"

I instantly recognized the profundity of the idea. Excitedly, I turned to Constance and told her that I was going to invoke Mercury by telling nothing but lies for the whole evening. "No you're not!" was her wise response.

I couldn't believe she did not see the magical genius of the idea. I argued that it would be the perfect invocation. "Every chance I get, I will lie! Mercury will love it. I'll be the only person there actually doing something purely mercurial." I told her. "Besides, it will be lots of fun!"

But Constance saw nothing perfect or fun about it. "I want nothing to do with it!" was her answer. "You're not going to do it!"

I finally gave in and said, "Okay. I won't do it."

(The invocation of Mercury had begun.)

We arrived a few minutes late. I apologized for our tardiness, saying that we had just returned from the cemetery where we had watched the exhumation of my father's body. Constance looked at me with silent disgust and found an excuse to get as far away from me as she could for the rest of the evening.

She's still mad at me!

Of course, everyone wanted to know why my father's body had been exhumed, and I was only too glad to tell them. It seemed that the family of my mother's second husband had been told by an acquaintance that my mother had bragged to a mutual friend about how she had poisoned my father. They took their suspicions to the police and finally got a warrant to exhume Dad's body for testing.

---

3 Traditions based on the mythological escapades of Mercury (the Greek Hermes) do indeed award to the wing-footed messenger of the gods the dubious distinction of being the god of liars, thieves, and lawyers.

Everyone at the party was enthralled by the story, which I told with a perfectly straight face. I even proudly pointed to the ring I was wearing that evening, and told them that I had been allowed to take it off my father's finger when they opened the casket.

Next, I told a few of the cast members how *hot* they looked in their Egyptian wigs and costumes, but I didn't get a chance to tell many more lies before the ceremony started. At the party that followed, however, I again became fully possessed by my lord Mercury. The lies dripped like quicksilver from my lips.

I started by announcing that our landlord had discovered that our house was contaminated with radon and that we had been forced to move to Garden Grove, where we now rented a large house owned by General Ky, the former prime minister of South Vietnam. I said it had a big backyard where we would be able to do initiations and produce the *Rites of Eleusis*—and that there was a rifle range in the basement. Everyone believed me!

You know, it's hard to keep up a constant stream of lies, even for me. In fact, I was starting to realize that it's impossible not to drag some element of truth into a lie. Actually I was starting to realize the inconstant and relative nature of reality itself—how there is no absolute truth, no absolute lies.

Was this the Mercurial revelation—the Mercurial trance of sorrow?

Try as I might to remain in character, the strain of all the lies eventually began to show. As the evening wore on (and it couldn't end fast enough for Constance) people began to suspect something was wrong with Lon's behavior. Our closest circle of friends became genuinely concerned. They cornered me in the kitchen just as I was reaching into the freezer for the bottle of gin.

"Lon, is there anything wrong? You're acting sort of strange tonight."

I looked at each of their sweet faces and it suddenly seemed the burden of the universe was about to be lifted from my shoulders. Every cheap movie confession cliché echoed now in my brain with Shakespearian gravitas... *"I can't go on living a lie!"*

This was a surprise payoff—a moment of unexpected spiritual bliss; a breathless moment when the feather of Maat quivers on tiptoe upon the scale-pan of judgment; the moment my answer would free me from the Mercurial *hell* that Constance knew I would create for myself with this stupid, harebrained idea. These people loved me. These people cared. I had toyed shamelessly with their feelings. I was ashamed, and so overwhelmed that I didn't know whether I'd be able to answer without choking up. I put down the bottle of gin, and looked each of them in the eye and confessed...

"My doctor told me I have a brain tumor."

Everyone gawked at me in stunned silence. People near the kitchen overheard and soon everyone at the party "knew" why I had been saying such outrageous things all night.

When Constance heard this last whopper, she could stay silent no longer. "He does NOT have a brain tumor! He's been telling lies all night because Mercury is the god of liars. Nothing he's said is true. I told him it was a stupid idea."

When the shock wore off, everyone else thought it was a stupid idea, too. Nobody, it seems, recognized the pure magical genius of my invocation of Mercury—nobody but me, of course. For a while I chalked it up to that *Curse of the Magus*[4] thing. Then I just realized pranks such as this are not what invocation is all about.

---

4 I, of course, am being facetious. "Magus" is the title of the initiatory level corresponding to Chokmah, the second Sephirah of the *Tree of Life*, and representative of the second-highest level of human consciousness attainable. Among many other obligations, the Magus is vowed to "... interpret every phenomenon as a particular dealing of God with my Soul."

||||||||||||||||||||||||||||||||||||||||||||||||||||||||||||||||||||||||||||||||||||||||||||||||||||||||||||||||||||||||||

TEN

... AND THAT'S WHAT
INVOCATION IS ALL ABOUT!

There is only one happiness in life, to love and be loved.

GEORGE SAND

Now that we know what invocation is not about, let's turn our attention to what it *is* about. In chapter 1, I mentioned the importance of invocation and the magician's personal relationship with the supreme intelligence (or the Great G). In this chapter and the one to follow, I'm going to share with you not only my thoughts on the matter, but also a ritual that has now become an integral part of all my formal magical operations. For many years, however, I missed the point of invocation entirely. For me, invocation was a cold and intellectual exercise—a necessary formality like doffing one's hat when entering a house of worship. I'm certain my attitude stemmed from the bad taste that lingered in my mouth from all the "invocations" I choked down as a lad growing up Protestant in

1950s Nebraska—a time when every service club barbecue, stock-car race, Cub Scout meeting, school[1] convocation, and football game was kicked off with something like…

> Heavenly Father, we call on thee to be with us here today as we gather ourselves on this athletic field of combat. Bless these boys,[2] their families, faculty, and friends who are here to witness the strength, courage, and determination of our proud Screaming Eagles and the godly man who coaches them. Bless our team and give them your strength as they battle for victory for the glory of your son. This we pray in his victorious Holy Name, Jesus Christ. Amen!

Please know that I am not ridiculing the concept of anyone acknowledging the presence of Deity prior to embarking on any serious and important undertaking. Indeed, by turning our attention "above," even briefly or halfheartedly, we connect something of ourselves with the universal source of creative energy. And honestly, who among us couldn't use a little shot of that kind of juice when we want our team to win, our fish-fry to sell out, our sermon to change lives, or our prayers answered?

But, even though magical invocations are (or at least should be) something dramatically different, most models presented to the modern magician (at least those examples that have come down to us from the magical adepts of the nineteenth century) are pretty damned boring too:

> Unto Thee, Sole Wise, Sole Eternal, and Sole Merciful One, be the praise and glory for ever. Who hath permitted me,

---

1 In the United States, praying out loud in public schools is now a no-no. But when I was in high school, every sporting event was opened with a Christian prayer of invocation.

2 When I went to school in the 1950s and 1960s, participation in organized athletic events (like military service) was pretty much reserved for the boys.

who standeth humbly before Thee, to enter thus far into the sanctuary of Thy mysteries. Not unto me, Adonai, but onto Thy name be the glory. Let the influence of Thy Divine Ones descend upon my head, and teach me the value of self-sacrifice; So that I shrink not in the hour of my trial. But that thus my name may be written on high, And my Genius stand in the presence of the Holy One. In that hour when the Son of Man is invoked before the Lord of Spirits and His Name before the Ancient of Days.[3]

In my rebellious and cynical mind, this Golden Dawn prayer and others like it are only slightly more magical than the pep-talk invocation bellowed through bourbon belches for the benefit of the proud Screaming Eagles. It would take me many years (and more than a bit of magical ripening) before I got it straight in my mind exactly who (or more precisely, what) I was invoking. Until then, my invocations remained breathtakingly anemic.

So, who *is* the "Sole Wise," "Sole Eternal," and "Sole Merciful One?" Who is "Adonai?" Who is the "Holy One?" When I stick my Solomonic magician's finger up into the great cosmic overhead electric light-socket of "above," who is the "above" I'm plugging my below-ness into? If it is the same abusive father-god of the great dysfunctional family of Chrislemews before whom I resentfully bent my boyhood knee, then "no thank you!" If it is the same phantom ear into which I superstitiously poured my teenage *quid pro quo* prayers for my girlfriend's menstrual regularity—if it is it the same ghost-god of birth-blinded nationalism in whose name every family, clan, tribe, and nation goes to bloody war—if it is the same all-powerful (yet curiously money-starved) god of oily televangelists—if it is the same might-and-white-is-right god

---

3 Israel Regardie. *The Complete Golden Dawn System of Magic. Vol. VII,* Third Revised Limited edition (Reno, NV: New Falcon Publications, 2008), 48.

of the fascist pundit or politician—or, indeed, if it is *any* god who would damn me for possessing common sense and daring to use it—then I most disrespectfully say, "Screw God!" I'm better off invoking my own *goddamned* common sense!

Eventually, I discovered that's exactly what I needed to do.

In the introduction to this book, I revealed that I "worship" a supreme consciousness that is the ultimate source of all manifest and unmanifest existence; and that I believe the ultimate nature of this super-existence is transcendently *Good*—a Good so all-comprehensively (and incomprehensively) infinite that there can be no-thing outside of itself—no "opposite" of this great Good. It swallows up all concepts of duality. If we could wave a magick wand and strip away all the superstitious absurdities and bigoted nonsense that infect most of the world's spiritual institutions, we would discover that this supreme consciousness, this Great G, is the true "God" of every religion.

The Great G is not the limited or parochial totem of any particular race or family or tribe or nation or culture or cult. The Great G is too big to be the purview of any cult or philosophy. In fact, the Great G is so big there is only one cosmic vessel capable of accommodating its more-than-absolute absoluteness. *And that's what invocation is all about*—squeezing the Great G into the only place in its own universe where it can fit—and that one place is *you.*

One would think that it shouldn't be too difficult to connect with the Great G. After all, it can never be anywhere other than completely within you and without you. There are, however, many obstacles preventing you from waking up to the reality that you already *are*, at this very moment, wallowing eternally in the infinite wall-to-wall bliss of Great G consciousness, and every one of those obstacles is also *you*! And that too is what invocation is all about—getting all the phony little "yous" out of the way in order to make elbow room for the Great G.

Unfortunately, all those phony little yous are pretty much everything you mistakenly think you are. But there is a fast and extremely effective way to burn away all the phony little yous and by doing so create the super-vacuum needed to suck in the glorious inrush of the Great G. It is a two-part magical technique is as old as human consciousness itself:

- The first part of the technique is the act of falling utterly, absolutely, unwaveringly, breathtakingly, helplessly, hopelessly, physically, mentally, emotionally, sexually, in love with God;

- The second part of the secret is allowing yourself to simultaneously receive *back* the same measure of love from God.

Like audio feedback created by a microphone that has been placed too close to the speaker of an amplifier, this simultaneous giving and receiving of love creates an ever-increasing feedback of bliss that is nothing less than the alternating electrical current of Great G consciousness—the current that joyously creates, sustains, and destroys the cosmos.

And *that's* what invocation is all about.

It took me a long time (over thirty-five years) to finally come to this realization. It came through the magical agency of a simple ritual which I will now share with you.

||||||||||||||||||||||||||||||||||||||||||||||||||||||||||||||||||||||||||||||||||||||||||||||||||||||||||||

ELEVEN

POP GOES GANESHA!

All around the mulberry bush
The monkey chased the weasel;
The monkey thought 'twas all in fun,
Pop! goes the weasel.

A penny for a spool of thread,
A penny for a needle—
That's the way the money goes,
Pop! goes the weasel.

TRADITIONAL NURSERY RHYME

I am now going to describe to you a little ritual that whirled into my bag of magical tricks about ten years ago. I first created it to be a whimsical meditation that I could quickly perform mentally to begin and end my morning routine, but it soon became for me something much more. In fact, within the context of its goofy simplicity, I have found not only a powerful banishing ceremony, but also a profound and breathtakingly effective technique of invocation. As it has become a key component to both my meditation and magical rituals, and because I will be referring to it in several places in the chapters that follow, I would like to share it with you now.

It is one thing to have an intellectual grasp and appreciation of the Great G, but it is quite another to allow oneself to gushingly melt in giddy adoration to it. I'll admit, as I was growing up I had a real problem loving God. No. That's not quite correct. I had a problem loving what seemed to be the monster everyone around me was calling God. Nevertheless, as I grew older I knew that if I was ever going to evolve into a sane and competent magician—if I ever hoped to perform a proper invocation, and become duly and truly connected with the divine "above," I would have to come to grips with my deep-seated negative attitudes. I would need to discover how to open my heart and fall in love with the Great G and set off the divine love feedback I spoke of a moment ago.

My first challenge was to settle on a tangible image, a form, a name for this formless and most abstract of abstract spiritual concepts. It would seem logical that I would try to personify the Great G in the likeness of one of the deities of my religion. After all, as a practicing Thelemite and archbishop[1] of my church,[2] my life is not bereft of gods and goddesses, foremost of which is a trinity of infinities that define the fundamental principals of Thelemic cosmology:

- *Nuit*—the Egyptian goddess of the night sky often depicted in Egyptian art as azure in color, tall and slender, arching over the earth. She is the infinity of an ultimately *expanded* universe (the circumference of the circle).

---

1 See chapter 13 and appendix 2.
2 Ecclesia Gnostica Catholica (EGC), the ecclesiastical arm of Ordo Templi Orientis.

- *Hadit*—Nuit's lover. In Thelemic/Egyptian iconography depicted as a winged solar disk. He is the infinity of an ultimately *contracted* universe, the point in the center of the circle. If Hadit were a phenomenon of physics I see him in his most fundamental character as the pre–Big-Bang singularity.

- *Ra-Hoor-Khuit*—the hawk-headed Crowned and Conquering Child of the union of Nuit and Hadit. Because Nuit's expansion (the infinite "out") and Hadit's contraction (the infinite "in") are both infinitely everywhere, so too must be their points of contact. This infinite contact creates Ra-Hoor-Khuit, a field of operation in which the universe can manifest.

Nuit, Hadit, and Ra-Hoor-Khuit are perfectly lovely cosmic concepts—awesome in fact—more than enough to qualify as proper deities to invoke. But, as much as I love my religion and the iconography of ancient Egypt, and as much as I respect these profound concepts, I personally find it very difficult (at least initially) to get emotionally warm and fuzzy at the thought of loving (and being loved by) the cold expanded universe, its dimensionless center, and the everything that lies between.

I also consider myself a hermetic Qabalist, and as such I worship the Great G as the threefold negativities that precede creation: *"Ain, Ain Soph,* and *Ain Soph Aur."* The concept of these three varieties of nothingness is as cool as modern jazz and (in my mind) catapults esoteric Judaism into the subtle stratosphere of Zen Buddhism (and vice versa). I sip my virtual espresso and snap beatnik fingers to applaud such hip transcendent realities, but honestly, how can I be expected to warm up to three wacky kinds of *nothing?*

If my magical career was to evolve, I realized I would need to find a sweet and simple god upon whom I could project all the infinite and sublime Great G concepts that already held my soul in jaw-dropping awe. I needed to gather all my infinites and omni-everythings (I'm making words up again) and bundle them to-gether into one irresistible and lovable package. And so, I set to work combing the pantheons of the world's religions, great and small, in search of a deity whose image and character resonates with my peculiar menu of spiritual programming. About ten years ago, I settled ever so comfortably on a deity that fills the bill per-fectly, the potbellied remover of obstacles, Ganesha.[3]

Ganesha

---

3 Alternately spelled *Ganesa* (and known in the East as Ganapati, Vinayaka, and Pillai-yar). Arguably, Ganesha is the best-known and most widely worshipped deity in the world. Hindus, regardless of sect or traditions, venerate the elephant-headed god, as do Jains, Buddhists, and millions of nonaffiliated devotees around the world.

Now, before you read anything unduly sectarian into my special relationship with Ganesha, I want you to know that I do not claim to be a devotee of Ganesha in the orthodox sense of the word. I do not belong to any Ganesha cults or sects. I don't travel to Ganesha pujas or festivals, nor have I memorized the 108 Names of Lord Ganesha (although they are wonderful beyond words).

Also, please be clear on this—I am *not* advocating that you or anyone else necessarily need to select the image, character, or concept of Ganesha as *your* tangible icon of the intangible, the supreme consciousness of the cosmos. It's your life, your spiritual cosmos, your magick. You are your own magician. Get your own God! If Ganesha floats your Great G devotional boat, fine! It's no business of mine or anyone else.

Everything I am about to describe in the following little banishing and invoking ritual can just as easily be applied using the character and image of any deity or object of your devotion—or any character or any *thing* of your choosing. I chose Ganesha because when I travel in vision to the throne-room of the supreme consciousness of the Great G, I can instantly and effortlessly imagine that I am beholding the all-loving and beautiful sweet face of Ganesha. My heart swells and overflows with a current of love for the divine, and I can joyously plunge my soul into the massive and cozy heart of that deity. But just as easily, I find myself totally receptive to that same flood of divine love and bliss coming from Ganesha, and therein lies the key.

Once I became comfortable with my new relationship with the Great G in the image and personality of Ganesha, I automatically began to acknowledge his presence and enlist his blessing and guidance prior to embarking on any serious undertaking. His huge ears were perpetually attuned to my prayers; his unjudgmental eyes lovingly bore witness to my noblest thoughts and deeds, and my vilest vices and vanities. At day's end, I comfortably rested in the folds of his great curled trunk as he rocked me to sleep.

Okay, I confess. I was dangerously close to becoming a Ganesha nut! (No offense to real Ganesha nuts). I even seriously thought about memorizing his 108 attributes, i.e., *Lord of the Whole World, Remover of Obstacles, Beloved and Lovable Child, Moon-Crested Lord, Master of Poets, Lord of Music, Huge-Bellied Lord* (Boy! Could I identify with a huge-bellied god!), *One Who Is Easy to Appease, Destroyer of All Obstacles and Impediments,* etc. But I'm a lazy man, and as my Lord Ganesha is easy to appease, I resolved that I would simply chant his name 108 times as a mantra prior to meditation or magick, or in the quiet moments before my lectures or musical performances, or indeed, before I did anything important.

A friend gave me a rosary of 108 beads[4] and for a while I used that to help me count off the "Ganeshas." Sadly, I ended up leaving it behind in an airplane seat somewhere between Copenhagen and London. I felt kind of funny using the rosary in public anyway, especially when I flew (and I fly a lot). Other passengers looked at me like I was some kind of white-haired terrorist saying my last suicidal prayers.

No. I needed a quick and easy way to silently and secretly chant the name of Ganesha 108 times while counting on my fingers. After much experimentation I discovered the perfect technique. I determined that if I sang the word Ganesh (or Ganesha) repeatedly to the tune of *Pop Goes the Weasel* I need only sing four and one half verses. Each full verse (example below) equals 24 repetitions of the Divine Name.

4½ verses = 108

---

4 I hope the reader will forgive me for not attempting to write another entire book on the subject of 108 and why the Hindus and others hold it in such veneration. One need only type "Why 108 beads?" on any search engine to begin your "never-ending" journey.

Ganesh Ganesh Ga-ne-esh Ganesh
Ganesh Ganesh Ganesh-a
Ganesh Ganesh Ga-ne-esh Ganesh
Ga—a—a—nesh-a.

Ganesh Ganesh Ganesh Ganesh
Ganesh Ganesh Ga—ne—sha
Ganesh Ganesh Ganesh Ganesh
Ga—a—a—nesh-a.

It works perfectly. I just keep track on the fingers of one hand. I can do it while driving the car. I can do it mentally while standing in line at the airport. I can do it while flying without alarming my fellow passengers, and, I eventually discovered, I could do it to both banish my magical circle and invoke the Great G.

In order for you to appreciate the simplicity of this little ritual, you need to understand the magical dynamics of how the magician moves about the temple in ritual in order to initiate and direct the flow of energy that either invokes or banishes a specific magical force.

INVOKING

(with the Sun)

In order to *invoke* (bring *in* the desired magical force), the general magical rule of thumb suggests that the magician move about the temple in a *clockwise* direction (i.e., around the perimeter or circle of the temple space, moving from east to south to west to north, returning to the east). This movement with the Sun's apparent daily path is called "deosil."

Standing in one place and spinning (rotating) clockwise is also considered an invoking movement.

Rotating clockwise (deosil) on one's axis also invokes.

The magician can also invoke by moving in a spiral pattern starting at the circumference of the temple circle and moving inwardly until coming to rest in the center—as if you were pulling the force or entity into the center of the temple.

Start

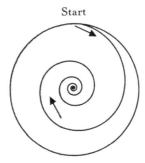

Movement in a clockwise (deosil) direction and spiraling inward invokes.

Naturally the power of this invoking movement is further amplified if the inward-turning spiral was performed in a clockwise (deosil) direction, and amplified even more if the magician was also performing deosil rotations while moving along the path of the inward-turning spiral.

BANISHING

(against the Sun)

Conversely, in order to banish (or send away), the general magical rule of thumb suggests movement about the temple in a counterclockwise direction (i.e., east to north to west to south, returning to the east). This movement against the Sun's apparent daily path is called "widdershins."

Standing in one place and spinning (rotating) counterclockwise is also considered a banishing movement.

Rotating counterclockwise (widdershins) also banishes.

By now you've probably surmised that you can also banish by moving in a spiral pattern starting from the center and moving widdershins outwardly until coming to rest at the far circumference of the circle—as if you were pushing everything out and away from the center of the temple. Naturally, the power of this banishing movement is further amplified if the outward-turning spiral is also performed in a counterclockwise (widdershins) direction, and strengthened even more if the magician is also performing widdershins rotations while moving along the path of the outward turning spiral.[5]

---

5 There are, of course, variations on this theme that magicians use to mix or match the dynamics of deosil and widdershins movements for specific magical effects. For this little ritual, however, we are applying them in the most simple and generic manner.

End

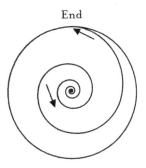

Movement in a counterclockwise (widdershins) direction
and spiraling outward banishes.

I call this little banishing/invoking ceremony "The Dance of Ganesha" and remind the reader it, like most other magical rituals, is much easier to actually perform and visualize than it is to read about it.

LIBER CVIII
THE DANCE OF GANESHA

A Ritual/Meditation

Part I. The Banishing

- The magician sits down in the center of the circle facing east, eyes closed. The entire ritual/meditation is accomplished in the mind's eye.

- Once relaxed and settled, the magician formulates in the mind a tiny living image of Ganesha[6]—standing in his colorful glory in the center of the magician's brain.

- Then, the tiny Ganesha bursts forth from the brain and stands on the floor directly in front of the magician. Magically, the image of the deity has now grown to about three feet high.

- Ganesha begins to gracefully whirl widdershins. (The image of spinning Ganesha should bring delight into the heart of the magician.)

- The magician now begins to chant the *Pop Goes Ganesha* mantra.

- While continuing to whirl widdershins, Ganesha now begins to *move* widdershins in an outwardly spiraling circle around the magician. (See figure on next page.)

---

6 Or the image of the deity or spiritual personage that represents the object of the magician's devotion.

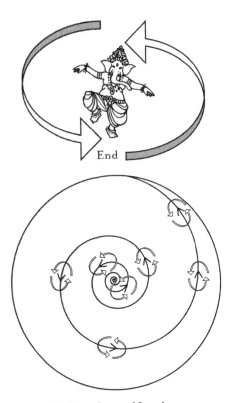

Banishing Dance of Ganesha

- As the spiral takes Ganesha farther and farther away from the center of the circle and the seated magician, the image of the deity grows in size.

- By the time the chant has reached the end of the first half of the first verse...

> *Ganesh Ganesh Ga-ne-esh Ganesh*
> *Ganesh Ganesh Ganesh-a*
> *Ganesh Ganesh Ga-ne-esh Ganesh*
> *Ga—a—a—nesh-a.*

...Ganesha's whirling spiral dance has brought him again directly in front of the magician, but by now the spiral has carried him to the far eastern limits of the temple room. The image of Ganesha is now about twelve feet tall.

- By the time the chant has reached the end of the second half of the first verse...

> *Ganesh Ganesh Ganesh Ganesh*
> *Ganesh Ganesh Ga—ne—sha*
> *Ganesh Ganesh Ganesh Ganesh*
> *Ga—a—a—nesh-a.*

...Ganesha's whirling spiral dance brings him again directly in front of the magician, but by now the spiral has carried him to the far eastern limits of the continent (in my case, North America). The image of Ganesha is now many thousands of miles tall.

- By the time the chant as reached the end of the first half of the second verse, Ganesha's whirling spiral dance has now encompassed the sphere of the earth and the orbit of the moon. The image of Ganesha is now hundreds of thousands of miles tall.

- By the time the chant has reached the end of the second half of the second verse, Ganesha's whirling spiral dance has encompassed the Sun and the orbits of all the planets in our solar system. Ganesha is now many millions of miles in size.

- By the time the chant has reached the end of the first half of the third verse, the dance has enclosed the Milky Way and Ganesha is now hundred of thousands of light years in stature.

- By the time the chant has reached the second half of the third verse, Ganesha's spiral dance has circumscribed the local group of galaxies in the neighborhood of the Milky Way. Ganesha is now millions of light years in size.

- By the time the chant has reached the end of the first half of the fourth verse, Ganesha's dance has reached so far into space that the Milky Way and our local group of galaxies look merely like one fuzzy star in the midst of billions of other star/galaxy groups. Ganesha is billions of light years in size.

- By the time the chant has reached the end of the second half of the fourth verse, Ganesha's spiral dance has pushed the physical universe to its inscrutable limits. There is no beyond. There is no size bigger. Space has been transcended. The concept of center and circumference has been obliterated. There is only the infinite immensity of Ganesha... and the infinite smallness of the magician seated in the deity's dimensionless center.

- The banishing is completed.

Part II. The Invocation

The magician has now chanted four complete verses of the *Pop Goes Ganesha* mantra. During those four verses, the ever-growing image of dancing Ganesha has banished (pushed away) the entire universe by whirling widdershins in a counterclockwise spiral until it has reached the limits of space-time. There is no more universe left for the now infinitely immense Ganesha to circumscribe—no outside of itself—not even empty space. When the magician has grasped the absolute immensity of this idea, he or she is now ready to invoke.

The infinitely large image of Ganesha standing before the magician now begins to gracefully spin clockwise. During the first of the four lines of the chant remaining, the spinning Ganesha will move in a very short inward clockwise arc until it enters into the magician's right ear. This movement completely drags the first quarter of the cosmos with it and deposits it inside the magician's own head.

Ganesh Ganesh Ganesh Ganesh

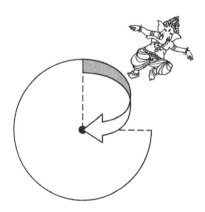

During the second of the four lines of the chant remaining, the spinning Ganesha moves in a very short inward clockwise arc until it enters into the back of the magician's skull. This movement completely drags the second quarter of the cosmos with it and deposits it inside the magician's own head.

Ganesh Ganesh Ga—ne—sha

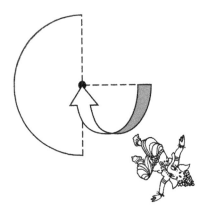

During the third of the four lines of the chant remaining, the spinning Ganesha moves in a very short inward clockwise arc until it enters into the magician's left ear. This movement completely drags the third quarter of the cosmos with it and deposits it inside the magician's own head.

Ganesh Ganesh Ganesh Ganesh

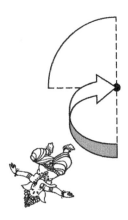

During the fourth and final of the four lines of the chant remaining, the spinning Ganesha moves in a very short inward clockwise arc until it enters into the magician's forehead. This movement completely drags the remaining cosmos with it and deposits inside the magician's own head.

Ga—a—a—nesh-a.

For a golden moment, the magician *is* Ganesha, the Supreme Intelligence, the Great G. There is "no outside" of the magician. The invocation is complete.

||||||||||||||||||||||||||||||||||||||||||||||||||||||||||||||||||||||||||||||||||||||||||||||||||||||||||||||||

TWELVE

THE RABBI'S DILEMMA

Divination is not a rival form of knowledge;
it is a part of the main body of knowledge itself.

MICHEL FOUCAULT,
The Order of Things

The reader who has come this far with me should by now have a fair idea of my basic magical field theory. It is with the most profound conviction that I embrace the words that form the subtitle of this book, "It's all in your head, you just have no idea how big your head is." This is not to say, however, that I believe magick is purely psychological. What I am saying is there is more we *don't* understand about the human mind than we *do* understand. With each new discovery we draw nearer to the realization that the mind is not limited by the brain. In fact, our brains, our bodies, our world, and even time and space are manifestations and aspects of mind. If we truly understood the limitless wonders of the mind and its relationship with the universal consciousness, we would know that in actuality there can be no *outside* of the mind—no outside of ourselves.

Does the mind explain everything? Theoretically, I'd say yes. But I would be the biggest liar in the universe if I were to even suggest that I am firmly in touch with that level of consciousness where everything is explained to me! And that's one of the reasons I find magick is so fascinating, and at times, so unexplainable. One does not need to understand every detail of the inner workings of a computer in order to install and operate a complex program. So too, the magician does not need to objectively understand every detail of the inner workings of the infinite mind in order to operate the system. I do feel, however, that in this day and age it is wise to give credit where credit is due, and woe to the sanity of the modern practitioner who would have others believe that he or she has guilefully cornered the market on understanding magical powers.

I reiterate all this because I am about to share two stories about magical operations I have done for the benefit of others. Such efforts when not considered carefully threaten to challenge my "it's all in my head..." field theory. After all, if "... the only thing I can change with magick is myself..." then how can I seemingly help others with my magical endeavors? Do I think that I am ultimately responsible for all the good and evil in the world?

I must confess, I'm not always clear on my own answers to those questions. But there is one thing upon which I am clear. Every bit of information that reaches the receptors of my senses and is processed by my brain—every myth I hear, every historical event I read about—every news story I watch—every book I read—every person I meet—every object, idea, image, sound, feeling, taste, emotion, observation, fear, or longing I encounter—*everything* changes me and becomes a living component of my conscious and subconscious reality. I am inextricably linked to everything that enters my realm of consciousness, and I am 100 percent responsible for how I process, react, and respond to it.

It might appear to the casual observer that my magick effects changes in the outside world. But ultimately, my outside world is one and the same as my inside world. If my magick does indeed bring about some desired change, it merely proves to me that somehow, someway, I have succeeded in transforming myself into the kind of person to whom such things happen.

In the spring of 2002, I received an e-mail from Ezriel,[1] a rabbi living on the East Coast, who wrote that he was familiar with my work and felt confident I could magically help him resolve a serious problem. In his first note, he did not describe his problem or what he wanted me to do. He said he wanted to simply introduce himself and provide me with personal information which he begged I would verify and keep confidential; this included his full name, address, professional titles, educational degrees, and details of his standing within an influential community of Orthodox Jews. He closed by restating his sincerity, and that he was willing to fly me to the East Coast, pay my expenses, and award me whatever my fee may be for "this kind of *black magick* work."

As you might imagine, I regularly receive letters and e-mails from some pretty colorful (sometimes very *disturbed*) individuals. I also occasionally receive requests from people asking me to curse an enemy, repel a psychic attack, expel a demon, extract an embedded extraterrestrial, or kindly endorse their claims that they are Jesus Christ, Aleister Crowley, or Cagliostro. I nearly always leave these requests unanswered, but Rabbi Ezriel's note struck me as being something more.

I took a few minutes and investigated on the Internet. I easily found a mountain of information about Ezriel's very ethnic home town. When I added his name to the search criteria, I found it prominently positioned among the religious and educational leaders of the community. I found it very odd that this pillar of piety

---

1 I am not using real names in this particular story.

would ask me to do anything of a black magick nature. Because he said he was familiar with my work, I assumed he was also familiar with the doctrines of esoteric Judaism. After all, nearly all the most popular systems of Western magick have as their foundation the Hebrew Qabalah. The term *black magick* wouldn't necessarily strike the same irrational terror in the heart of an esoteric Jew as it would in that of a mainstream Chrislemew.

I was intrigued, so I cautiously e-mailed him back and inquired about the details of his problem. His response was immediate and poignantly candid. His only son, David (who himself was a rabbi), had been married for nearly two years and had not yet become a father. David and his wife, Sarah,[2] had been examined by physicians who found them both to be in good health and capable of conceiving a child. After giving me a short and breathtakingly politically incorrect lecture on the religious and cultural importance of his son having a child (especially a boy), he repeated his offer to immediately bring me to the East Coast and pay me to do whatever was necessary to make his daughter-in-law pregnant.

After I banished from my vulgar comedian's brain a thousand crude and sophomoric possible responses to this statement, I took a day to gather my thoughts and ponder how I should respond to this offer. I hope the reader appreciates the fact that I am not a wealthy man. I connive and struggle day-to-day and month-to-month, just to pay the rent for our little duplex and pay the extortion fees to the blood-sucking organized crime cartels that pose as American health insurers. Try as we might, in our forty-two years of marriage, Constance and I have never been able to rise above the station of genteel poverty. I confess the thought of taking financial advantage of this situation did indeed cross my *lumpenproletariat* mind.

---

2 Actually, Ezriel never felt it necessary to tell me his daughter-in-law's name, referring to her only as "my son's wife."

The next morning I wrote back and answered as honestly as I could. I insisted it would not be necessary for him to bring me to the East Coast or for him to come to California, and that I would be happy to freely offer my magical advice. I frankly stated, however, that I thought it would be unwise for me to attempt to magically intrude in the lives of his family in this manner.

He responded within minutes insisting that, on the contrary, he most certainly *did* want me to magically intrude—specifically, he wanted me to call up a demon of the Goetia and command it to make Sarah pregnant.

I replied to the effect that even if I were willing and able to raise a fertility demon, and Sarah did become pregnant and give birth to a baby boy, there would be serious and unavoidable psychological consequences for both the child and his family. I asked him to realize how, like in a fairy tale, the blessing would soon turn into a curse—how the happiness that would first accompany the child's birth would soon be overshadowed by the nagging fear that every illness, every accident, injury, or misfortune visited upon the child throughout his lifetime was somehow the evil result of the demonic black magick operation that had engendered his nativity.

The rabbi coldly responded, "I am willing to take such a curse upon myself."

I had to admire the depth of this man's resolve. Such fearlessness and focus may characterize a fool, but are also the mark of a natural magician. I was beginning to realize Ezriel had already set into motion the magical forces that would make Sarah pregnant, and that my participation had already become in his mind a factor in the equation. I resigned myself to try to help him in any way I could. I was sure, however, that raising a Goetic spirit was not going to be the way to do it. I wrote him back and told him so, adding that I was prepared to consult with other spirits to determine the facts of the matter and how best to proceed. He seemed satisfied with that, and thanked me.

I don't know how he would have felt had he learned that the "other spirits" to which I referred were those who oversaw the operations of humanity's oldest[3] continually consulted oracle, the Chinese Book of Changes, the *I Ching*.

For those of you not familiar with this marvelous oracle, I must apologize for being unable to offer a proper introduction. Instead I must direct you to the many fine translations of the text, which can be found in bookstores worldwide. My favorite is one by Richard Wilhelm and rendered into English by Cary F. Baynes. It has an excellent foreword by Carl Jung and is a real treasure for lovers of Eastern mysticism in general and the *I Ching* in particular.[4]

I have been an *I Ching* dilettante since the late 1960s. I am not being overly modest when I stress my amateur status; for me to suggest otherwise would be a most outrageous presumption. It is said the great Confucius waited until he was ninety years old to study the oracle, and wrote that if he had another ninety years to devote to its mysteries, it would not be enough time. I have discovered, however, that even a superficial familiarity with the images suggested by the ever-changing lines of its sixty-four hexagrams can provide profound insights into questions and issues ranging from the mundane to the sublimely spiritual. For the answer to the rabbi's dilemma, the *I Ching* was to be the only "spirit" I would trust with this most personal and sensitive issue.

Before dinner that evening, I showered and put on my most comfortable magical vestments (clean black sweatpants and sweatshirt). I took my Wilhelm/Baynes translation from the top shelf of my bedroom closet and unwrapped it. (Tradition suggests that

---

3 The roots of the *I Ching* can be traced back to Ching's legendary first emperor Fu His (4000 BCE).

4 *The I Ching or Book of Changes*, translators Richard Wilhelm and Cary Baynes. (New York: Bollingen Foundation Inc., 1950). Third edition reprinted with corrections by Princeton University Press, 1969.

when not in use, the oracle should be stored high above one's head, and wrapped in white silk.) I placed it on a small table near the south window of my bedroom temple. I lit a stick of incense and placed it in a holder and tray on the floor just north of the table.

I knelt before the table and bowed three times, each time lightly touching my forehead to the floor. I would remain kneeling throughout the entire process, a gesture which at the time was for me not accomplished without some measure of pain. I hoped the rabbi would appreciate this!

I unwrapped a bundle of fifty dried yarrow[5] stalks and, holding them in my right hand, rotated them clockwise three times in the incense smoke while I asked the question out loud: "What is preventing David and Sarah from conceiving a child?"

I removed one stalk from the bundle and laid it horizontally in front of me as a reminder of the supreme consciousness. Then, for the next fifteen minutes (in obedience to the rather complex traditional procedure) I carefully manipulated the remaining forty-nine stalks to randomly generate the number groupings that would create a stack of six lines (called a hexagram).

Each of the six lines of the basic hexagram is either an unbroken line (male—yang) or a broken line (female—yin). There are thus sixty-four ways possible ways to combine six lines that are either broken or unbroken. To the ancient Chinese sages who developed the system, these sixty-four different hexagrams presented to their minds archetypal images that in turn suggested ideas, situations, even moral commentaries on historical, social, political, and personal matters.

---

5 Yarrow is also known as woundwort or nosebleed. Its medicinal properties have been known for millennia in both the East and West. Traditionally, yarrow has been associated with I Ching divination since the earliest years when sacred tortoises were released in a temple courtyard "planted" with a grid of dried yarrow stalks. The pattern of the stalks the tortoises knocked down was then interpreted for the answer to the question.

These ideas are not static. Indeed, like everything in our objective reality, the hexagrams are in a constant state of change (hence the name, "Book of Changes"). Consequently, depending upon the nature of the answer, any one of the six lines of any given hexagram may be in the process of changing (or "moving") into its opposite. In other words, each line of the hexagram can be one of four varieties:

- An unbroken line (male—yang)
- A broken line (female—yin)
- An old unbroken line (a male so old it will soon change/move to female)
- An old broken line (a female so old it will soon change/move to male)

The text of the *I Ching* provides specific commentaries for each hexagram and for each of the "moving lines" of the hexagrams. For the reader who may feel hopelessly confused at this point, let me just briefly summarize:

While it is possible, using the traditional yarrow stalk method, to arrive at a hexagram containing no moving lines at all, in most cases, the person asking the question receives the answer in three stages:

- The primary hexagram (and its commentary) that usually paints a picture of conditions surrounding the present situation.
- The commentary (or commentaries) on the moving line (or lines), which usually points to the aspect of the situation that is currently changing, or is about to change.
- The new hexagram (and its commentary) that is formed when the moving line (or lines) have changed/moved into their opposites. This part of the answer is usually the most suggestive of what the "future" might hold.

I liken the process to viewing three consecutive drawings on one of those flip cartoons we used to make with a pad of paper when we were kids. The viewer can't understand the plot or message of the cartoon by simply looking at each individual drawing. The plot is revealed by sensing the apparent progressive movement of the images when several pages are flipped before our eyes.

As in all divinatory systems, the answer is ultimately revealed through the agency of one's own intuitive impressions. Almost without exception, the *I Ching* speaks to us in metaphoric language (like a fortune cookie on steroids) that rings true only if we are attuned to hear the answer from out of its flowery prose.

To my great relief, the *I Ching* answered my question—*What is preventing David and Sarah from conceiving a child?*—in a remarkably clear manner. It came as a classic three-part answer made up of:

1) The primary hexagram (No. 9), which is called The Taming Power of the Small;

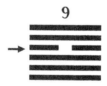

2) with moving line 4 (from the bottom), which transforms the primary hexagram into...

3) Hexagram 1, which is called, The Creative.

Now it doesn't take a seer to see that the ultimate answer to my question (the third and final step in the process) was hexagram 1, the most "male" of all the hexagrams. That being the case, it was pretty clear to me that David and Sarah would indeed succeed in becoming parents and that it was highly likely that the firstborn would be a boy. Furthermore, the appearance of Hexagram 1 as the third and final part of the answer seemed to suggest that the eventual birth of this particular child would be a particularly profound event:

> ...When an individual draws this oracle, it means that success will come to him from the primal depths of the universe...[6]

This, however, did not answer the question of what was currently preventing David and Sarah from conceiving and bringing forth this child and what change would occur to make this happen.

Looking back at the first part of the answer, Hexagram 9, The Taming Power of the Small, we see that most of the ingredients for a successful conception, pregnancy, and birth (dense clouds) are in place but there was yet no rain:

> The Taming Power of the Small has success. Dense clouds, no rain from our western region.[7]

The text continues at length and these are a few of the highlights that jumped out at me:

> ...Hence the image of many clouds, promising moisture and blessing to the land, although as yet no rain falls...Only through the small means of friendly persuasion can we exert any influence...To carry out our purpose we need firm de-

---

6 *I Ching,* 4.
7 *I Ching,* 40.

termination within and gentleness and adaptability in external relations.[8]

The commentary on the moving line (the fourth line from the bottom—the line that when changed turns Hexagram 9 into Hexagram 1) says:

If you are sincere, blood vanishes and fear gives way. No blame.[9]

Now, I'm certainly not a marriage counselor, and I couldn't say for sure if it was David or Sarah who was going to need to learn a lesson in "gentleness and adaptability in external relations," but it sure sounded to me like there was the real presence of fear in the relationship and *somebody* was not exceeding by romantic delicacy. In any case, if David had inherited even a small measure of his father's somber insensitivity and inflexibility, Sarah just might be under a lot of emotional pressure—perhaps even enough to prevent conception. Perhaps a small change in David's attitude or behavior could neutralize his anxiety and her fears long enough to solve this problem. The *I Ching*'s commentary on the Image seemed to agree:

The wind drives across heaven: The image of THE TAMING POWER OF THE SMALL. Thus the superior man refines the outward aspect of his nature.[10]

Okay. That was enough for me. My "spirits" had spoken. I was confident that Sarah and David would have a son, that Ezriel would be a grandfather, that the ageless traditions of that East

---

8 *I Ching*, 40–41.

9 *I Ching*, 42.

10 *I Ching*, 41.

Coast fairy-tale community would go on at least one generation more—if David could just become a "superior man" and "refine" the outward aspect of his nature... in bed.

I wrote Ezriel. I told him I had consulted with my spirits and that I was assured a man-child would be born to David and Sarah if David made the effort to be gentle and charming to Sarah prior to making love. I then really stuck my neck out and added, "The child will be conceived the moment they lie laughing in each others' arms." To tell you the truth, I don't know why I added that last part. It just came to me like I was momentarily possessed by some *Fiddler on the Roof*-type character.

I immediately got an e-mail back thanking me for my help, but no other comments. I then worried that my answer was too corny or personal or unmagical (or perhaps too *Fiddler on the Roof*-ish) to be taken seriously.

About sixty days later, I received a very upbeat message informing me that Sarah was pregnant and that everyone was hoping for the best.

About six months later, I received an e-mail from the Rabbi proudly announcing the birth of his grandson, and the simple note, "Thank you for your efforts."

|||||||||||||||||||||||||||||||||||||||||||||||||||||||||||||||||||||||||||||||||||||||||||||||||||||||||||||||||

THIRTEEN

THE EXORCISM OF
OUR LADY OF SORROWS

PART I

A School Possessed

I don't fear Satan half as much as I fear those who fear him.
Saint Teresa of Avila

Perhaps the most dramatic example of Low Magick (at least as we are defining the term in this book) is the art of exorcism. Exorcism reaches back into prehistory, and, together with rites of fertility and the hunt, vies for the title of humanity's oldest spiritual practice. Writing about exorcism is in its own way as dangerous as exorcism itself—perhaps more so, as there is so much opportunity for serious misunderstanding, not to mention all the evils ignorance and fear can visit upon superstitious humanity.

For young magicians, dabblers, and dilettantes the fantasy of waging magical war with a hideous demon who has taken up residence in some tormented soul reeks with the prospect of heroism, spiritual romance, and adventure. In truth, more often than not, where the subject of exorcism is concerned, the whole sad business merely *reeks*.

As I feel I must keep reminding you, I am not a mental health expert nor do I have a degree in psychology, so please understand that my opinions on this subject are drawn purely from a magical perspective and from my experiences with individuals who have solicited my advice and/or assistance (some of whom I felt actually needed an exorcism, though most of whom I believe did *not*).

Let's bear in mind that the science of mental health is still in its infancy, and that in centuries past, maladies such as epilepsy, schizophrenia, depression, dissociative identity disorder (a.k.a. multiple personality disorder), and countless other conditions both mental and physical were believed to be the result of supernatural causes. The ancient physicians who attributed certain physical and mental abnormalities to demon or spirit possession might not have been so off the mark, especially when we remember that their patients' spiritual reality included a solid belief in spirit illness and demon possession. Even today, rather than viewing a disease as our body's natural reaction to an unhealthy lifestyle, chemical or biological poisoning, or an inherited abnormality, we apply a personal face to the malady as a malicious enemy that needs to be resisted and battled and defeated.

The wise witch doctor, shaman, or physician of old knew that if one could first heal the mind, the body would likely follow. If in the patient's mind the illness could be simply personified as a common garden-variety demon—a bothersome pest that could be driven off by a skilled exorcist—then the immense negative energy of the patient's own fear and superstition could be turned back upon itself and used as a positive force to alleviate the illness. Inspired by healings chronicled in the New Testament,[1] modern faith healers still effectively apply variations of this prehistoric art upon ailing members of their flocks whose spiritual worldview is similarly superstitious, simple, and absolute.

In this place, however, I am not going to regale you with tales of exorcisms or faith healing, or even exorcisms in which (and whereby) an alleged discarnate entity or spiritual force is driven from the body and mind of an afflicted individual. Instead, I'm going to share with you the story of the exorcism of a school whose faculty and students were visited by a disturbing string of tragedies.

It would be improper (indeed, unwise) for me here to reveal the actual name of the school[2] or the city or state where it is located. I will tell you that it is an Archdiocesan high school for girls that has been administered for more than one hundred years by a particular group of Dominican Sisters; and that I was retained by the principal of the school (who I will refer to as Sister Martha) under circumstances that I am now about to relate.

Before I go any further, however, I must pause and remind the reader that the Roman Catholic Church has a formal Rite of Exorcism[3] that (in rare occasions and under the direction and authority of a bishop) is performed to cast out demons and evil spirits à la the popular film *The Exorcist*.[4] There are several reasons the rite is so infrequently employed today; one of them likely being the modern

---

1 Matthew 9:22, 15:28; Mark 5:33–35; Luke 8:42–49; Acts 14: 8–10. See also my book *Accidental Christ: The Story of Jesus as Told by his Uncle* (Chicago: Thelesis Aura, 2006).

2 I here call it "Our Lady of Sorrows." That is not, however, actually the name of this historic school.

3 The liturgical text of the exorcisms in the Roman Ritual was written in 1614; it was revised following Vatican Council II. A "New Rite for Exorcisms of the Roman Ritual" was presented by Cardinal Jorge Medina in 1999.

4 *The Exorcist*. Warner Brothers, 1973. Book and screenplay by William Peter Blatty.

Church's discomfort with something that appears so embarrassingly medieval, with another being the miles of ecclesiastical red tape involved in proving to the Church's satisfaction the necessity for such a radical confrontation with the Prince of Darkness.

The criteria for such proof are very specific and involved. If, however, the evidentiary hurdles are cleared, it can take additional time to find a bishop willing to authorize the procedure, and (if the bishop is unable or unwilling to do the job himself) to find an exorcist capable and willing to perform it. It often takes years to get a first-rate Roman Catholic exorcism on the road. More often than not, by then the possessee has gotten better (or has died most colorfully) before the exorcist walks out of the theatrical fog and comes knocking at the door.

The reason a bishop is required to perform (or order) an exorcism springs from the Christian tradition that bishops are supposedly possessed of a kind of magical electricity that evil spirits hate, fear, and cannot resist. The Church, of course, doesn't refer to this power as being "magical," but when they describe the nature of this force, one can conclude it can be nothing else *but* magical. They maintain that this current is passed from individual to individual by the laying on of hands with full intent to transmit it. In other words, one bishop makes another bishop by laying his hands on another man[5] and saying something to the effect of, *"John Doe, it is my intention to make you a bishop, and so I'm going to lay my hands on you and pass some of my magical electricity on to you. It's okay…I can make more."*

Supposedly this magical juice comes down through an unbroken chain of guys who were touched by a guy who was touched by a guy who was touched a guy, etc., etc., back to the first century to a guy who was touched by a guy who was touched by *Saint Peter.*

---

5 Bishop making has nearly always been a *man* thing in the Roman Catholic and Orthodox churches.

Please don't think I'm being unreasonably disrespectful when I observe that Peter, despite his other admirable spiritual qualities, was according to the Gospels probably the stupidest of the disciples of Jesus. How stupid was he? He was *so* stupid that during a rare outburst of exasperation, Jesus called him a "rock." Contrary to the absurd interpretation concocted in the Dark Ages by an understandably confused and embarrassed church, calling someone a rock in first century Palestine was not a compliment. In Aramaic, "rock" is a most insulting epithet. It doesn't mean, "I think you're *heavy, man*," it means, "I think you are an *idiot*—as dense and stupid as a stone!" Jesus goes on to say something to the effect that it would be on such immovable rock that the whole future church would be built.[6] (Obviously, in this instance, Jesus is proven to be a great prophet!)

This chain of magical electricity from Saint Peter to the modern bishop is called apostolic (as in *apostle*) succession. Like electricity, the power (real or imagined) is in itself neutral. Once you have it, you have it. It cannot be taken away. If the Church dared to admit such power could be taken away then they would have to also concede that it wasn't all that powerful in the first place. Ultimately (and technically) one's membership in the Church (indeed, in any church) has nothing to do with it. Faith or morality or personal piety or virtues have nothing to do with it. If you were touched by a person that has it—and if they touched you with full intent to pass it on—then you have it, too. Just like *cooties*!

I realize that all this talk of bishops and magical electricity might seem a departure from the more colorful subject of this chapter, but I want you to know this so that you may understand one of the reasons I was retained to exorcise a Roman Catholic school.

6 Matthew 16:18.

The fact is that even though I am not a Roman Catholic or an Orthodox Christian, I possess the bishop cooties too!

The circumstances that conspired to confer this curious distinction upon me are interesting, but would take us even farther afield from the subject of this chapter. Suffice to say, I am a bona fide bishop possessed of legitimate apostolic credentials from at least thirty lineages traceable to Saint Peter or one of the other apostles of Christ.[7] I think it important for you to know, however, that I do not believe that being so consecrated imbues me (or anyone else) with extraordinary spiritual merit or magical power. Like anyone else on this planet, any virtues or magical powers I may or may not possess are borne of the caprice of my inherited destiny and my own efforts toward spiritual evolution. They are certainly not the result of being touched by a long string of guys who were originally touched by *Peter the Idiot.* Sister Martha's spiritual worldview, on the other hand, obliges her to believe otherwise.

But I'm getting ahead of myself. Here's how events unfolded.

It began with a conversation my brother Marc had while giving a healing treatment to his Reiki instructor. For reasons even Marc cannot explain, he is a naturally powerful healer. (Please see appendix 1 for more background information on Marc's unique ability.) I tease him that his *chi*[8] basket is broken and he spills the subtle energy everywhere he goes. Be that as it may, whenever his teacher falls ill, Marc is the only practitioner he allows to work on him. During the course of the treatment, Marc's teacher mentioned that his sister is a Dominican nun (Sister Martha) and that she is the principal of Our Lady of Sorrows high school in a nearby

---

7 See appendix 2. Those of you for whom such things matter will be interested to know that the consecrations to which I refer in this place come from apostolic lines other than those I also possess in my capacity as archbishop of Ecclesia Gnostica Catholica, the ecclesiastical arm of Ordo Templi Orientis.

8 Chi (or qi) the active principle or energy flow of life. Similar to the concept of prana in yoga.

city. It is one of the oldest Catholic girls' school in the state. She had recently complained to him how psychically unhealthy the old school building seemed to "feel" and asked him if he knew someone who might come in and give the building a good spiritual cleansing. He told his sister-the-Sister that he did indeed know someone whom he believed radiated an extraordinary amount of good energy and recommend she contact Marc.[9]

Sister Martha called Marc and he agreed to come and give the school a good once-over. Several nights later, he was left alone in the building for the entire night. He systematically walked through and "cleansed" each room on every floor. It was nearly dawn before he finished. Sister Martha contacted him several days later and thanked him, adding that the building "felt" much better. That seemed to be that, and Marc didn't hear from Sister Martha until she called him again, a little over a year and a half later, to tell him something terrible was happening at the school.

She went on to describe a string of misfortunes and tragedies that had befallen the staff, faculty members, and their families in the last thirty days. It started with a car crash in which a young administrative assistant and her baby were burned to death. A few days later, a teacher, a man in his late forties, announced he had been diagnosed with pancreatic cancer. He died within a week. The maintenance man severed a finger. The accountant fell and broke her hip.

The staff was soon talking of a curse, and the more they talked, the worse things got. Every day brought a new and terrifying event: a broken bone, breast amputation, unexpected illness, murder or suicide in the family. To add to the litany of personal tragedies, the school building itself was starting to "act" strangely. Teachers

---

9 You might think that this conversation sounds very New Agey and subjective, but let's remember these two siblings grew up in an environment that allowed one to become a Roman Catholic nun and the other a New Age healing practitioner.

arrived in the mornings to find desks moved and papers strewn on the floor. A fluorescent light tube in a classroom ceiling burst, scattering shards of glass upon the heads of students. The entire administration had become paralyzed with fear. In whispered conversations in the teacher's lounge, they crystallized their collective terror and superstitiously personified the horrible chain of events as an attack by the devil himself.

For the students, the most horrifying and traumatic event occurred just hours before Sister Martha phoned my brother. Sister Catherine, the school's most beloved and popular teacher, a vibrant young woman in her mid-twenties with no known health issues, collapsed in her classroom and died in the throes of a grotesque and violent seizure before the eyes of her terrified pupils.

Sister Martha was truly frightened and admitted frankly that she believed there was an evil presence in the school that needed to be exorcized. Marc confessed that exorcisms were a bit out of his line but said that his brother was a ceremonial magician and a consecrated Gnostic bishop who had participated in several exorcisms in the past. Sister Martha asked Marc to please contact me and see if we might be able to come to the school that night.

Marc called me and repeated as much as he could. As you might imagine, this was something that interested me very much. I asked him to call Sister Martha and tell her we would both come and meet with her, and, if agreeable, stay the night in the building.

I hung up the phone and I sat for a moment wondering what I had gotten myself into. How would I go about exorcising a school building? What was it exactly that I'd be exorcising? It's my firm conviction that *all* schools are haunted, especially high schools which, even under the most ideal circumstances, are seething swamps of chaotic sexual energy created by decades of confused and tormented adolescents. Hell! *I* still haunt the halls of my old high school and junior high! In dreams and nightmares, I find myself running late to a class, unable to remember the time of day or room number. Sometimes I find myself climbing the stairs or trapped somehow between the walls of unremembered hallways. High schools are ghost traps—even for the living!

How much more intense the energy must be in a very old Catholic girls' high school where year after year, decade after decade, its spooky icon-festooned chambers are crammed with hundreds of girls all undergoing the mystifying metamorphosis into womanhood—all generating the immense and unpredictable psychokinetic energy that accompanies the uniquely female mystery of the first issue of blood. It is with good reason that, when investigating hauntings and paranormal phenomena, the first question the professional investigator asks is, "Is there a menstruating girl or woman in the house?" The premise of Stephen King's novel and film *Carrie* is not that much of an exaggeration.

And so, I was not at all surprised that the school building itself was capable of snagging and enraging a malignant force. What I didn't as yet know was exactly what that force was. Furthermore, I needed to figure out what magick formula would be appropriate for an operation such as this.

My mind was spinning too fast. I needed to pull myself together. I needed to ground myself. I needed to enter sacred space—a telephone booth to God—a place where the true omniscient "me" talks and the not-so-omniscient me listens. As it happened, I knew of just such a place—and it was just a few steps from my telephone. I stripped off my clothes and stepped into *the shower*.

There, where the blessed hot water descends like the Holy Spirit from my crown to my toes—while my hands busy themselves with the automatic routine of the bath—while my brain runs on automatic pilot and my senses are engaged by familiar smells and sensations, my mind is released to listen to the great intelligence of which my own is merely the small and opaque reflection.

I have composed entire songs in the shower. I have conceived books in the shower. Month after month I figure out how I will *pay the rent* in the shower! And that afternoon, before the hot water turned cold, I knew precisely how I would go about exorcising Our Lady of Sorrows high school.

PART II

Preparation

Father Damien Karras: "I think it might be helpful if I gave you some background on the different personalities Regan has manifested. So far, I'd say there seem to be three ..."

Father Merrin: "There is only one."

The Exorcist[10]

It has been my observation (always in hindsight) that the real "magick" of a magical operation is accomplished in the preparation process rather than the execution of the ceremony itself. The magick ritual is merely the seal that grounds the current of the magician's will and completes the circuitry on all planes.

Like Minerva leaping from the cloven skull of Zeus, my plan for the exorcism was fully formed before I stepped out of the shower. It crystallized in my brain in the timeless moment between the shampoo and rinse, and was triggered by a simple vision—a childhood memory of old Mr. Jacobs, the janitor at my old elementary school,[11] sweeping the floor of the gymnasium. His technique was simple, methodical, and tidy. He would first sweep all the dirt and debris from every corner of the gym floor and concentrate the mess into one neat pile in the center of the floor. Then, with a final flourish of the broom, he dispatched the nasty pile into his dustpan.

I would do the same. I would sweep the totality of the phenomena—the entire conglomerate of forces and energies that were tormenting the school and its inhabitants—into one pile, and then I would treat that pile as a single spiritual entity. I would focus and

---

10 *The Exorcist* (see chap. 13, n. 4).

11 Highland Park Elementary School, Columbus, Nebraska. I remember Mr. Jacobs having long, curved fingernails as thick as an eagle's talons.

create one master devil that embodied all the lesser demons that severally worked their specific acts of mischief and terror—one spirit that I would evoke into the Solomonic Triangle of art. Once I had the nasty critter trapped, I would have a proper talk with it, banish it, curse it, and if necessary, annihilate it using the tried-and-true techniques of the art of Solomonic magick.

You might think this somewhat presumptuous of me. After all, where does DuQuette get off creating demons? Aren't there already enough evil spirits running around the cosmos? I confess these questions didn't even occur to me, because for all intents and purposes the staff, faculty, and students of Our Lady of Sorrows had already created the devilish spirit. They just didn't know its name. And, for the moment, neither did I.

What's in a name? It is a universal axiom, promulgated by the magical traditions of nearly every age and culture, that discovering the name of a spiritual entity gives the magician power over it. Recall the story of Rumpelstiltskin. In traditional Solomonic magick or Goetia, the names of the seventy-two spirits are provided in the text.[12] The book also contains the images of each spirit's "sigil" or seal. The seal is a very important ingredient in the recipe of evocation. Indeed, it is upon the seal in the Triangle that the spirit appears before the magician.

Two copies of the sigil are used in the classic ceremony: one is drawn on a medallion that is worn around the magician's neck; the other is drawn on parchment and placed within the Triangle where the spirit will appear. The magician and the spirit are thus linked by the two sigils. The spirit is drawn to its own sigil, and then becomes trapped in the Triangle while the magician stands in the relative safety of the Circle. I'll talk more about that in a moment.

---

12 Crowley, *Book of the Goetia*, 27–64.

My first task would be to discover the spirit's name, and then use the letters of its name to generate the image of its sigil, which I would use in the operation. Other magicians I'm sure will have their own ideas about how this is best done. On this occasion, I chose to use the pendulum. Over the years I've gained some proficiency applying this marvelous tool in magical and divinatory operations. My pendulum is a small brass plumb that was given to me many years ago by my dear friend Donald Weiser. It is attached to a string about eighteen inches in length. I use it in a variety of ways, but for this task I would use it to determine a series of "yes" or "no" questions—a clockwise rotation indicating "yes" and a counterclockwise rotation indicating "no."

I went to the garage and got down the family's Scrabble[13] game, opened it up, and emptied the lettered tiles on the living room coffee table. I turned the tiles face down on the table and swirled them around for a moment. I then tied the string of my pendulum to the tip of my magick wand and began the process of selecting the letters that spelled the name of the demon.

It must have been quite a scene—a large man in a black robe sitting on the couch and dangling his wand and pendulum like a tiny fishing pole over each Scrabble tile while asking out loud to (seemingly) no one in particular, "Is this a letter in the name of the demon of Our Lady of Sorrows?"

About ten minutes later, the pendulum had chosen only three tiles, which I set aside (still face down) while I put the rest of the tiles back in the box. Then, one by one, the pendulum determined the order of the three letters in the spirit's name. I then turned the tiles over and, voilà! The name was revealed.

It was a funny looking name with no vowels: S L G. Would that be pronounced Slug? Slog? Slig? Sloog? Slyge? Sludge? I had

---

13 Scrabble is made by the Hasbro company.

to admit "Slug" sounded like a perfectly proper and nasty name
for a demon. If these were Hebrew letters, they would probably
be ס (Samekh), ל (Lamed), and ג (Gimel). Each Hebrew letter also
represents a number. In this case Samekh = 60; Lamed = 30; and
Gimel = 3. Together they total 93.

Now, 93 is a pretty important number for many modern hermetic Qabalists who, like me, subscribe to the magical doctrines
of Thelema,[14] and the watchwords *"Do what thou wilt shall be the
whole of the Law"* and *"Love is the law, love under will."* If you've
ever corresponded with a Thelemite, you've perhaps noted that we
begin our letters and e-mails with the former phrase and close with
the latter. The words "will" and "love" in Greek are "thelema" and
"agape" and each enumerate to 93. In informal communications
and in social settings, Thelemite magicians often abbreviate these
phrases to their numerical essence and simply greet each other
with a friendly, "93."

This amused me at first, as if the demon were being playful. My
amusement soon cooled as it occurred to me that the "S" in the
spirit's name could also be treated as the Hebrew letter ש (Shin),
whose number is 300, and in that case the name Sh L G would
add to 333.

I realize that not everyone reading this book is a magician or a
hermetic Qabalist, and therefore should not be expected to appreciate what all the fuss is concerning these numbers. But, for many
modern magicians, no number carries more terrifying implica-
tions than does 333. It is the number of the archdevil Choronzon,
the dweller in that horrible pathless *anti-region* of the Tree of Life
known as the Abyss.

---

14 From Wikipedia: "Thelema is a philosophy or religion based on the dictum, 'Do
what thou wilt shall be the whole of the Law ... Love is the law, love under will,' as
presented in Aleister Crowley's *Book of the Law*—Liber AL vel Legis. The word is
the English transliteration of the Koine Greek noun θέλημα: 'will,' from the verb
θέλω: to will, wish, purpose."

Every magician, as he or she ascends the evolutionary ladder of consciousness, is sooner or later obliged to pass through the looking-glass of this Abyss. It is the final barrier preventing the true essence of the magician's consciousness from identifying completely with that of the Divine. The ego cannot make it through the Abyss; indeed nothing that the magician has heretofore considered "self" can pass through that awful non-place. If the "crossing" is successful, what emerges on the other side is the equivalent of a Buddha—a Master of the Temple—a level of consciousness represented by the third Sephirah, Binah, on the Tree of Life. If unsuccessful, the magician (still clutching to and identifying with the false self of ego) falls into the Abyss and is lost in the perpetual madness of a "false" Sephirah, Daath, closed off and separated from both the divine influence from above[15] and the merciful distractions of mundane consciousness from below.[16]

Now, before any of us gets too carried away here, I want to make it perfectly clear that I presently dwell conspicuously low on the Tree of Life's initiatory ladder of consciousness. I do not believe that I was on that day, nor am I now, poised upon the precipice of that great initiatory crisis. But at the time I did interpret the numbers 93 and 333 to be an unmistakably personal two-part message to me from the demon, which I will vulgarly and succinctly boil down to something like this:

- "93"—*Hi Lon. I've got YOUR number, Mr. Hot-shot Thelemic Magician!* and
- "333"—*Don't mess with me. I'm one bad-ass demon!*

---

15 The Supernal Triad of the Tree of Life, Sephiroth 1, 2, and 3 (Kether, Chokmah, and Binah).

16 The seven Sephiroth below the Supernal Triad of the Tree of Life, Sephiroth 4, 5, 6, 7, 8, 9, and 10 (Chesed, Geburah, Tiphareth, Netzach, Hod, Yesod, and Maluth).

I'm not going to attempt to further explain the magical nuances implied by the manifestation of these numbers as they relate to the demon's name and my own magical career; neither do I wish to overstate or overdramatize the significance of either number 93 or 333 in this particular context. It is enough that you understand that for me this bit of Qabalistic information added a new and disturbingly personal spiritual dimension to this operation—one that informed me in no uncertain terms that the struggle in which I was about to engage was inextricably linked to unseen and unrecognized issues relating to my own initiatory journey—indeed, it was my battle, my crisis, my initiation. Sister Martha didn't know it, but in asking me to exorcise Our Lady of Sorrows she had also retained me to call forth and exorcise a demon from myself. When you think about it, how could it be otherwise?

As for the true and proper name of the demon, I decided to incorporate both spellings and call it SLG-ShLG,[17] pronounced Slug-Shlug (very Lovecraftian, I thought).

I created a simple Slug-Shlug sigil by using the large lettered rose from the center of the Hermetic Rose Cross.

---

17 In Hebrew, שלג-סלג = 426 the same number as מושיע = "Savior" from Isaiah 45:15, "Verily thou art a God that hidest thyself, O God of Israel, the *Savior*."

Hermetic Rose Cross

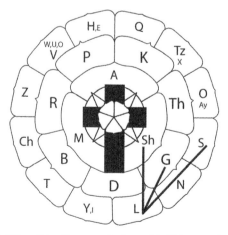

Sigil of Slug-Shlug Drawn on the Rose of the Hebrew Alphabet

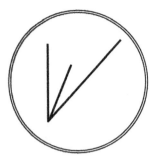

Sigil of Slug-Shlug

Sigil of Slug-Shlug within the Triangle of Evocation
Drawn on a yellow 3 × 3 Post-it Note

Now that I knew the spirit's name and had its sigil, I used a Magic Marker to draw the sigil on the front of a circular copper medallion. The medallion was attached to a chain. I would wear it around my neck and show it to Slug-Shlug immediately upon its appearance in the Triangle, thus binding it to me for the duration of the ceremony. Etched on the reverse side of the medallion is the image of the Pentagram of Solomon. It is the symbol of the microcosm and the magician's mastery of himself (or herself) and the world of the elements. It is the second image the magician displays to the spirit on its appearance—sort of like a police officer show-

The Pentagram of Solomon

The Hexagram of Solomon

ing his or her badge to the bad guy. It is also a handy thing to flash if the spirit becomes obstinate... or worse.

I drew another version of the sigil within a triangle on the top sheet of a new pad of yellow 3 × 3 Post-it Notes. I will soon explain why I used a Post-it Note for this purpose. For now, please be satisfied with knowing that I would place this pad in the Triangle during the ceremony of evocation, and that it would later play a prominent role in the exorcism itself.

I now had everything I needed to evoke the demon Slug-Shlug. Marc was due to pick me up in less than two hours. I needed to work fast. This would not be a straightforward evocation whereby I simply evoke the spirit, introduce myself, give it its assignment, then order it to run along like a good fellow and do its duty. On this occasion, I was to do something that I had never done before, even in my past capacity as exorcist. This time I would formally conjure the spirit at *one* location (my home), then, without dismissing it from the Triangle, and without me stepping out of the protective precincts of my Circle, I would transport my activated temple (including myself inside the Circle and the demon inside the Triangle) to another location (Our Lady of Sorrows high school). There, in the middle of the night, I would resume the operation and proceed with the exorcism.

I will now describe how it was done.

PART III

Preliminary Evocation

"...for his Robe hath he not a nightdress; for his instrument a walking stick; for his suffumigation a burning match; for his libation a glass of water?"

LIBER ASTARTÉ[18]

I'm afraid the following description of my hurriedly composed and extempore evocation of the demon Slug-Shlug will be somewhat of a disappointment to magicians (and would-be magicians) who are enraptured by the glamour of the elaborate trappings of the ancient art of evocation. I assure you that in the last thirty-five years, I have on many occasions taken great pains to adorn myself with the *most proper* vestments, arm myself with the *most proper* weapons, and erect the *most proper* pieces of temple furniture (including a *most proper* Circle and Triangle festooned with the *most proper* divine names and words of power). The essence of the structure is hard-wired in my psyche and I dare say I could reconstruct the essential setup in my dreams. Now that I think about it, I have on occasion done *just that*.

For this working, however, I needed to operate quickly and under extraordinary conditions. My working area and weapons by necessity needed to be spartan and portable. These are the consecrated[19] magical items I used on this occasion:

- A wand of almond wood seventeen inches in length.

---

18 The magician consecrates each of his or her magical tools in a separate ceremony that takes the object through a series of steps that largely mirror the landmarks of the ritual of initiation. The object is treated as the candidate. It is banished, purified, and charged with its specific duty; then anointed with the Holy Oil and dedicated exclusively for magical purposes. All the items I use to evoke spirits, no matter how simple or improvised they may be, have been so consecrated.

19 If by chance you have not read this chapter, please do so now.

- A thin silken cord approximately eleven feet long. When the ends are tied together and it is laid out on the floor, it forms a circle approximately three and a half feet in diameter.
- A carpenter's segmented ruler which, when its segments are fully extended and then folded into three equal segments, forms a perfect triangle of twenty-two inches per side.
- The copper medallion (with chain) bearing the seal of Slug-Shlug on the front, and the Pentagram of Solomon on the back.
- The Post-it Note with the image of the seal of Slug-Shlug within a Triangle.
- A clip-on juror's badge I once "accidentally" wore home from jury duty. To this ill-gotten prize I glued a paper image of the Hexagram of Solomon. The Hexagram is clipped to my robe to display to the spirit that I have made an unbreakable link with the macrocosmic deity, and that I am operating under the auspices of the Most High.

For the evocation ceremony itself, I wore a purple yarmulke on my head, and my plain black robe, over which I hung my bishop's stole—a long, wide band of richly embroidered material that hangs around the back of the neck and falls over the front of the body. My stole displays on its wide red and gold bands images of the Greek Cross, the Eye in the Triangle, the descending dove, and the Holy Grail. Later, for the exorcism at the school, I would wear the yarmulke and the stole over street clothes (black slacks, white dress shirt, and a plain black tie).

I quickly cleared a space on the floor in my office (itself a Herculean labor akin to that of cleaning the Augean stables). I banished and purified the temple pretty much as I described in chapter 6. I unfolded and arranged the carpenter's ruler to form a triangle and placed it on the floor. I put the Post-it Note pad bearing the sigil of the spirit in the center of the Triangle. (Please remember, the image on the Post-it Note also contains a Triangle within which the sigil is drawn.) I placed a stick of burning incense in a small burner in the Triangle next to the sigil. I tied together the ends of the silk cord and arranged it on the floor to form a crude Circle. My Temple was ready.

I sat down in the Circle, wand in hand. I took a moment to gaze into the Triangle at the yellow Post-it Note sigil of Slug-Shlug. Everything looked comically serene—the demon's sigil resting there next to the stick of burning incense, its tiny red coal politely spitting up an undulating serpent of smoke. I closed my eyes and proceeded to mentally chant my Ganesha mantra and visualize the cosmic banishing/invocation dance I described in chapter 11. As always, the exercise did its magick. In just a few moments I was infinitely centered. I opened my eyes with the realization that contrary to all appearances there was no "outside of myself"—that I was one and the same with the Great G.

Once thus firmly connected with the *above*, I proceeded to connect with the *below*. I aimed my wand directly at the spirit's sigil and conjured Slug-Shlug into the Triangle.

Most modern Solomonic magicians use the *Lesser Key of Solomon*[20] as their guidebook and script for evoking spirits. It is filled with page after page of addresses, conjurations, cures, and greater curses designed to cajole, threaten, or otherwise terrorize an unwilling spirit into the Triangle. I believe, however, that these hypnotic and rambling speeches do not really serve to bamboozle the spirit into the Triangle, but rather, are designed to bamboozle the *magician* into confidently believing he or she has the full authority, power, and ability to do it! That afternoon my conjuration was extremely loud and very, very brief.

---

20 Crowley, *Book of the Goetia.*

"Slug-Shlug! Come!"

I was oddly awakened by the sound of my own words. It was as though I had commanded every dog in the universe to "Sit!" and they had no choice but to obey. It must have been pretty loud, because a bird that had been minding its own business outside my office window was startled into flight. The sound of its fluttering wings instantly summoned into the Triangle of my mind's eye the image of a huge Norwegian magpie.

Again, I was surprised to the point of distraction. I have seen these marvelous birds many times on my visits to Norway and England. They are more audacious and mischievous than crows or ravens, and because of their thieving habits and reputation for eating the eggs and babies of other birds, they are held in superstitious awe by many European cultures. In England, the appearance of a single magpie is an omen of great evil that can only be warded off by respectfully saluting the solitary bird.

"I'm here," it squawked.

"I salute you," I answered.

Such conversational exchanges with demons are difficult to describe because the answers from the spirit enter the mind of the magician on the same brainwaves that carry the questions. The bird cocked its head to the side and dipped a quick bow of acknowledgement. I held up the copper medallion and showed the spirit its sigil.

"Do you see this?"

"I see it."

"What is it?"

"My mark," it answered coldly. I turned the medallion around and showed Slug-Shlug the Pentagram of Solomon.

"Do you see this?"

"I see it."

"What is it?"

"The mark that binds me."

I held up the juror's badge with the Hexagram of Solomon glued on it.

"Do you see this?"

"I see it."

"What is it?"

"The mark that binds you!" it said sarcastically.

These answers satisfied me. It was now time to put the operation on ice.

"You will remain in the Triangle. I will visit you again soon. Do you understand?"

"I understand."

"Swear it!"

Then, as much as a talking bird can, it cleared its throat and said, "I swear. I will remain in the Triangle."

Without further conversation or ceremony, I stood up within the Circle, removed my yarmulke and stole and stripped off my robe. I then carefully gathered around me the silken cord of my Circle, wrapped it tightly around my naked body, and tied it securely in place. I would not take off the medallion or leave this Circle until the exorcism was accomplished.

PART IV

Interview with Sister Martha

The doors of heaven and hell are adjacent and identical.

NIKOS KAZANTZAKIS,
The Last Temptation of Christ

I quickly dressed (concealing my silken magick Circle and medallion under a clean white shirt and black tie). I jotted down a few notes in my magical diary (including a hastily composed "oath") and threw it in my briefcase along with a few other items necessary for a traveling exorcism:

- My almond wand (wrapped in its red satin bag)
- My yarmulke
- My bishop's stole
- A vial of Oil of Abramelin (see chapter 6)
- The yellow Post-it Note pad with the sigil of Slug-Shlug permanently trapped in its own little Triangle
- A flask of "Holy Water" (see chapter 6)
- Two fresh votive candles and a glass candleholder
- Two cigarette lighters
- Six sprigs of fresh rosemary (clipped from our backyard herb garden)
- The lid to a medium-sized saucepan

Marc arrived to pick me up, and soon the *DuQuette Brothers' Traveling Exorcist Show* was on the road to Our Lady of Sorrows high school. It was early evening and the campus was closed when we pulled up to the towering Spanish wrought iron gate. Marc pushed the security button and announced our presence to the voice in the black box. Just as if in a proper gothic horror movie, the gates groaned open and we drove through.

Sister Martha stood outside the door on the side of the main building and indicated where we should park. She was a rather small woman in her mid-forties wearing a black skirt and simple gray suit jacket over a white blouse. I was disappointed she was not decked out in full medieval drag. Still, if I were asked to pick out the nun in a room full of women, she'd have been my choice.

After introductions, Sister Martha gave us a brief tour of the building, pointing out the locations of various "supernatural" manifestations as we went along. We spent several minutes in the classroom that witnessed the death of young Sister Catherine, and the tour ended at the faculty lounge and the administrative staff area.

The lounge seemed innocuous enough, but I was immediately disturbed by the layout of the staff area, which was reminiscent of the nightmarish set designs of early German expressionist films. It was an asymmetrical and chaotic maze of misshapen cubicles completely devoid of clean right angles or unobstructed lines of sight. The office of the vice principal was the only enclosed office; its large windows provided a perfect overview of the panorama of chaos.

I am by no means an expert on feng shui, but I couldn't help but think this entire area was surely a serious impediment to any kind of energy flow—a severe case of *chi* constipation if I ever saw one!

The whole scene would have been comical had it not been so overpoweringly claustrophobic and suffocating. The area was accessible by only one door that opened onto the hallway. Just standing there made me gasp for air and want to run away, but it was here that Sister Martha lingered as she related details of the specific tragedies and misfortunes that had recently befallen the poor souls who labored for their daily bread in that warped little trapezoidal hell.

She had, in fact, prepared a one-sheet dossier (complete with name, age, picture, job title, and the sad details of each victim's particular affliction, accident, or tragedy), which she clipped to the hanging in-box attached outside each victim's door or cubical entrance. For example:

> *Jane Doe—34—accountant—(picture)*
>
> *Fractured arm while recovering from breast surgery. Office formerly occupied by Janet Doe who perished with baby in car fire.*

Marc and I were impressed.

Before she left us to our work, we sat down for a few minutes in her office to chat. She told us that she had been busy all afternoon arranging the school's memorial service for Sister Catherine. She was visibly upset and very tired. She told us we would have access to the entire building up until 6:00 a.m. when people would start arriving for the next school day. There would be only one other person in the building during the night, Larry the IT man, who did his computer duties at night.

She rang Larry in his office and asked him to please come to her office. When he appeared, Sister Martha introduced him to Marc and me and told him we would be in the building for several hours during the night doing "some work" for her, adding that we had her permission to go anywhere in the building and that he was not to disturb us.

Larry was a gaunt man, perhaps forty years old, in jeans and a dark gray T-shirt. He seemed a bit high-strung, and I got the clear impression that he viewed us with suspicion.

"What kind of work?" Larry asked nervously.

"Nothing at all to do with your computers, Larry. They won't be disturbing you," Sister Martha quickly interjected before either Marc or I could respond.

Larry did not appear satisfied with Sister Martha's answer. He looked at Marc and me as if he hoped we would offer more information. When none was forthcoming he stammered, "Well, I'll be backing up the system all night so if they want to look at…"

"They'll not be working with the computers, Larry," said Sister Martha with a tinge of irritation in her voice.

I quickly decided I didn't like Larry. When he disappeared, Sister Martha told us how to lock the building and gave us the security code to open the gate. She then thanked us again for coming, presented us with a check (a very generous figure, we thought, for such an intangible service), and said she'd leave us to our work. She opened her handbag and was fishing for her car keys when her cell phone rang. She plucked it from her purse, flipped it open, and answered.

"Yes dear. How are you doing?" She obviously knew the caller.

Then after a long moment of silence, Sister Martha sat down and sighed, "Oh dear, when? Is anyone with you?" She listened silently for a couple of minutes more before saying, "We are all praying for you, dear. Try to get some rest. I'll see you tomorrow."

She flipped her phone shut and glared blankly at Marc and me.

"That was Sister Catherine's mother. Her husband, Catherine's father, was devastated by her death. He collapsed and died about half an hour ago."

For an uncomfortably long moment it seemed that Sister Martha was going to say something more. She didn't. She picked up her purse and keys.

"I'll let you get started now."

PART V

The Exorcism

What an excellent day for an exorcism!
REGAN, FROM *The Exorcist*

Marc and I were in a pretty somber mood after Sister Martha left. Marc said he would like to systematically go through the building as he had done previously and when he was finished would wait for me in the faculty lounge. I told him I would more or less follow in his wake. We conferred for a few minutes in the hallway as we confirmed our respective routes through the school.

As the faculty lounge would be our base camp and final meeting place, we agreed we would both start there. I waited in the hallway while Marc did his thing. When he was done, he went on his way and I reentered the lounge and prepared myself for the magical marathon to come.

I sat down in the most comfortable chair in the room and put my briefcase on my lap. I closed my eyes, took a couple of deep breaths and repeated my Ganesha banishing/invocation mantra and visualization. Then I reluctantly got up out of my comfy chair, loosened my tie, unbuttoned the collar of my shirt, and fished out the medallion bearing the image of the Pentagram and the sigil of Slug-Shlug. I arranged it so it neatly hung over my tie. I then re-buttoned my collar and slid the knot of my tie trimly against my throat. For some reason, I felt it was vitally important for me to appear as "professional" as possible. I opened my briefcase and again anointed my head with a tiny dab of Oil of Abramelin, popped on my yarmulke, clipped my juror's badge hexagram to my shirt pocket, and put on my bishop's stole.

For the first time, I noticed the life-sized and obscenely gruesome crucifix hanging on the wall near the bulletin board. How could I have missed that? I moved closer to have a better look. Surprisingly, my dark cynicisms regarding the church and Christianity in general disappeared, and for a moment I saw the Great G in that ghastly symbol. I looked into the helpless eyes of God and uttered this thirty-three-word oath.

I, Tau Lamed[21] swear by everything I hold sacred, that I will not leave this building until I have exorcised the spirit that torments this school and those who labor and study here.

I lit the small votive candle and turned off all the other lights in the room. I then removed my wand from its bag and proceeded to banish, purify, consecrate, and seal the room in the following manner:

- With the wand, I performed the Lesser Banishing Ritual of the Pentagram.

- With the wand, I performed the Lesser Banishing Ritual of the Hexagram.

- I purified the room by sprinkling the four quarters with holy water, and announced, "This room is purified with water."

- I consecrated the room by approaching the four quarters with the votive candle in hand. With it, I "drew" an equal-armed cross in the air at each quarter, and announced, "This room is consecrated with fire."

- I suffumigated the room by approaching the four quarters with burning rosemary, which I kept igniting from the flame of the votive candle that I carried from quarter to quarter on the lid of the saucepan (which also served as my ashtray).

---

21 Tau Lamed (or T. LMD) is my ecclesiastical name and motto. The Hebrew letter ל, Lamed, is spelled למד, Lamed, Mem, Daleth (LMD), the initial letters of my name.

- Returning to the center of the room, I placed the forefinger of my right hand against my lips and took a deep breath. I then forcefully expelled my breath as I swept my hand down in front of me and to the side and back of my body as I shouted, "*Apo pantos kakodaimonos!*" (Greek for "away [and/ or behind me] evil spirits!")

- Upon leaving the newly banished, purified, and consecrated area, I sealed the room by dabbing Oil of Abramelin on my fingertip and "painting" a pentagram upon the inside of the door, and three Tau Crosses (**T**) on the outside of the door (one each on the left, right, and upper door posts).[22] As I drew the Tau Crosses, I whispered the words, "*In nomine Babalon Amen. Restriction unto Choronzon!*"[23]

For the next two and a half hours, I systematically repeated these seven steps in every room and hallway of the building I could access. The second to the last area I cleared in this manner was Sister Martha's office and its adjoining bathroom. I remember thinking she must be a truly good person. Her office was a sane and calm oasis in an otherwise troubled and disturbed universe. I wanted to linger there, but it was getting late and I knew the most difficult part of the evening was still before me.

I sealed Sister Martha's office with three sweet cinnamon-scented crosses and crossed the hallway to descend into the feng shui hell of the administrative staff area. The place seemed even more terrible than it had just a few short hours ago. I performed the full seven-part ritual inside each tiny cubicle, pausing to read each dossier. It

---

22 I did this in imitation of the lamb's blood sprinkled on the doorposts to prevent the angel of death from visiting the Egyptian homes of the mythological Children of Israel.

23 I consider these the most powerful words of protection that can be uttered by a magician of my particular religion.

was very difficult (and a little dangerous) wending my way by candlelight through the maze of desks and chairs. After over an hour the smoke from all the burning rosemary became so thick in the enclosed area that I feared it would set off the smoke alarm system. Mercifully, that did not happen.

I came at last to the semi-private office of the vice principal. Here I would resume the evocation that I had put "on ice" so many hours ago back home. Like old Mr. Jacobs, the janitor in my vision, I had swept the filth of the entire building into one neat pile.

I chose this area for the final showdown for several reasons. First, it had the most room for me to work. Second, all of its walls (including the one with the door and windows that opened to the common area) reached from floor to ceiling. It seemed like the nerve center of the problem and the perfect venue to trap a demon. Lastly, I have to confess, I took perverse pleasure in remembering how in my rambunctious school days I had confronted several other rather obnoxious demons in a high school vice principal's office.

Those of my readers who are experienced magicians can imagine my state of mind after spending so many hours of banishing, etc. Even simple ceremonies such as these raise a remarkable amount of energy and require an intense level of concentration just to hold the visualizations in place. I was physically exhausted yet at the same time psychically energized. Very few times in my magical career had I reached this exalted level of spiritual intoxication. By the time I reached the VP's office, the borderline between the material and the magical worlds had essentially vanished. To say I was hallucinating would be an understatement. For hours now, my pentagrams and hexagrams had hung visibly in the air around me, and each time I spat out the words, "*Apo pantos kakodaimonos!*" every spirit entity, good or evil, went scurrying off to anywhere in the building that had not been cleared and sealed off by the wild-eyed exorcist. The only place left for all that concentrated smutch to take refuge was here—and the air in the room hung thick with the stinking demonic chum of the entire building.

I slapped Slug-Shlug's little Post-it-Note sigil and Triangle on the desk pad of the VP's desk and stepped back a few feet. I checked to make sure I was still wearing my yarmulke, magical juror's badge, and the medallion bearing the pentagram and the demon's sigil. Lastly, I patted the outside of my shirt to assure myself that I was safely wrapped in my magical circle. Everything being in order, I aimed my wand at the Triangle and commanded as before, "Slug-Shlug! Come!

Slug-Shlug appeared immediately—quietly, peacefully, as if only a moment had passed since our last encounter—a large, handsome Norwegian magpie perched pleasantly upon his yellow Post-it Note. I marveled at how normal it all seemed. I was almost happy to see him, grateful for his exotic and dangerous companionship amid this cowed and colorless *hell* of a Catholic school. His presence made the evening come suddenly alive and interesting.

Like a fool, I initiated a conversation.

"Why do you torment these people?"

"Is it evil for the crow to feast upon the eyes of a dangling knight?"

Right now, as I'm writing these words, they appear on the page to be melodramatic and corny, like something pulled from a demonic fortune cookie. At the time, however, they sounded anything but corny. In fact, Slug-Shlug's response took my breath away. In my fevered brain, the allusion was unmistakable. The demon was describing the doom of the luckless Knights of the Round Table who failed in their quest for the Holy Grail; they were hung from trees like obscene fruit, and their eyes were plucked out and eaten by crows.

I didn't answer—at least, I didn't make a conscious effort to answer. I stood accused by my own tidy spiritual worldview—paralyzed by the paradoxes of my smug philosophy. Indeed! Who was I to presume to understand and judge the rightness or wrongness of the tragedies of Our Lady of Sorrows? Were not little *goods* and little *evils* both parts of the Great G "goodness" of the supreme consciousness? Had I plumbed the depths of the souls of these people? Had I weighed their infinitely complex karmas—their inherited destinies—and found some profound miscarriage of cosmic justice that only Lon Milo DuQuette could put right? Did I think I was some knight in shining armor galloping down the freeway to save the fair nuns and children? Was my clarity of vision so superior that I could, with ego-driven impunity, tamper with the momentum of life and death of hundreds of people I've never met? Indeed! *Is it evil for the crow to feast upon the eyes of a dangling knight?*

Why was I here? What really was my motive for doing this? Why was I standing here with my almond wand and my holy water and my magick toys and my purple yarmulke and my pretty bishop's stole? Did I look cool? Did I think all this was going to look impressive in my magical diary? Maybe I'd even write a book about this someday!

These thoughts triggered in my exhausted brain a chain reaction of even more crippling doubts and self-recriminations—all as the great bird grew more noble and stately as it stared silently at me from within the Triangle of my magical mind's eye. But then, I realized that he *wasn't* being silent, and that the accusatory voice I was hearing was that of the demon and not my own inner soliloquy. It was the damned magpie that tormented me with these thoughts, these ideas, these images.

I had to hand it to Slug-Shlug; this was classic demonic behavior and I had fallen for it hard. My concentration had been severely broken and as soon as I realized what was going on, Slug-Shlug started to flap his wings and lift himself into the air. I brandished my wand toward the Triangle as if I were snapping a whip.

"Back down! You son of a bitch!"

Every ounce of will flowed through my extended arm and out the barrel of my wand. It took everything I had to bring the great bird down upon the Triangle. The moment his talons touched down, I heard a noise outside in the hallway. Out of the corner of my right eye I saw the door to the staff area suddenly swing open.

"Oh! Sorry!" was all Larry the IT man could say after barging into a smoky, candle-lit room to find a red-faced wizard in a yarmulke and a bishop's stole aiming a stick at a tiny yellow Post-it Note.

I did not move; neither did I take my eyes off the Triangle. With the same strange voice that called forth Slug-Shlug, I snarled at poor Larry through gritted teeth, "You're going to have to *leave,* Larry!"

Larry left.

That did it! No more talking to Slug-Shlug. I didn't care any more why I was doing this. I didn't care whether or not I was here because of my ego or my insecurities or my karma or my duty or my goddamned spiritual quest. Screw my motives! Screw good and evil! I was here, doing what I was doing because the universe had conspired to put me in this place. That was enough! The momentum of *my* life put me here and I wasn't going to leave until the job was finished. There would be no attempts to redeem this spirit. I would not fart around trying to cajole, torture, banish, exile, or otherwise attempt to reprogram this monster into an "angel of light." I was insanely angry—filled with a rage that exploded from my heart and arm, and through the death-ray gun of my wand.

I would not abide its existence for one second longer. I took fiendish delight in spitting out the most hideous curse in my arsenal of Solomonic curses:

Christeos cormfa peripsol amma ils! ("Let the company of heaven curse thee!")

Christeos ror, graa, tofglo aoiveae amma ils! ("Let the sun, moon, all the stars curse thee!")

Christeos luciftia od tofglo pir peripsol amma ils, pujo ialprg ds apila, od pujo mir adphaht! ("Let the light and all the Holy Ones of Heaven curse thee, unto the burning flame that liveth forever, and unto the torment unspeakable.")[24]

Slug-Shlug dissolved without a squawk. I felt as though my body was set in stone, my arm and wand still leveled at an empty desk. Oddly enough, I did not feel triumphant, or even relieved. My overall feeling was that of embarrassment over the fact that I had allowed the spirit to toy with me, and that I had not simply annihilated it immediately upon conjuration.

I composed myself for a moment or two, then performed the seven part banishing procedure and sealed the vice principal's office. I took the *Post it Note* Triangle (with the departed spirit's seal) into Sister Martha's bathroom, burned it, and flushed the ashes down the toilet. I packed my gear back into the briefcase and joined Marc who was waiting for me in the faculty lounge.

---

24 *The Goetia—The Lesser Key of Solomon the King—Clavicula Salomonis Regis. Translated by Samuel Liddell MacGregor Mathers.* Edited with an Introduction by Aleister Crowley. Illustrated second edition with foreword by Hymenaeus Beta (York Beach, ME: Samuel Weiser, 1996), 118.

PART VI

Post Mortem

The belief in a supernatural source of evil is not necessary;
men alone are quite capable of every wickedness.

JOSEPH CONRAD

Marc and I treated ourselves to a couple of bottles of water as we debriefed in the faculty lounge. Neither of us shared many details of our labors. I did mention that Larry had burst in on me at the climax of my conjuration. We giggled uncomfortably for a moment, then fell silent as we both realized that Larry's office was the only place in the building neither of us had worked on. At that moment the door opened and Larry poked his head in.

"Sorry if we bothered you, Larry." I said with more than a hint of sarcasm.

"I just wanted to make sure you guys were all right. What was it that you were doing?" Larry was visibly agitated. Marc shot back an answer.

"Just helping out Sister Martha. You'll have to ask her for details."

"Well, if it has anything to do with the computers, I'm doing a backup tonight and it will take a while."

"Nothing to do with your computers." I told him. "And we're done for the night." Larry said nothing in response. He just lingered in the doorway for a moment as if unsure what to do or say next.

Marc and I were indeed done for the night. We were both very tired. I wanted nothing more than to get home, take a long shower and sleep all day—which is pretty much what I did. I woke up early in the afternoon and in the cold light of day replayed the events of the night before in my mind.

I was generally pleased with the exorcism and harbored little doubt that I had magically done everything I was capable of doing. However, I was convinced that Sister Martha would need to address a couple of very serious issues if the school was ever to become psychically healthy—the most obvious (and the easiest to correct) being the layout of the administrative staff area. I would be completely remiss in my exorcist's duty if I neglected to advise Sister Martha in the strongest terms to immediately hire a commercial feng shui consultant to rearrange the area.

My second concern would be more difficult to address head-on, because it dealt exclusively with my own very personal and subjective impressions. I had to be very careful as to how I would go about advising Sister Martha on this issue; I'm referring, of course, to the issue of Larry.

Please don't misunderstand me. Not in my wildest magical fantasies did I suspect Larry was consciously some kind of Satanic minion—a "Renfield" to Slug-Shlug's Dracula. I had no reason to believe that he was anything more or less than a harmless IT nerd doing his best every night to make a living. But his insecurity, paranoid behavior, and willingness to defy Sister Martha's instructions led me to question, at the very least, his personal integrity and emotional stability. I am not a mental health expert, and my impressions are totally subjective, but Larry's conduct and demeanor left me with the distinct impression that he was a very disturbed man; and very disturbed men make effective conduits, capacitors (condensers), storage batteries, and *amplifiers* of magical and psychic energy.

You may beg the question, "Did the evil school building make Larry crazy, or did crazy Larry make the school building evil?" It does not matter. Larry was likely every bit a victim as Sister Catherine, or the maintenance man who cut off his finger. As a magician, however, I cannot ignore the obvious. When I conjured the demon Slug-Shlug by name, Larry-the-IT-man walked into the room. Larry was in all likelihood an unwitting cog in the great nightmarish machine that was Slug-Shlug. I strongly believed that for the good of the school, and for Larry's own good, he should be removed from that environment.

I called Marc, and we discussed our conclusions. Marc then called Sister Martha and told her that the staff area needed a feng shui professional to rearrange things. Being inclined to embrace New Age concepts, she enthusiastically agreed and said she would do that immediately.

Marc then mentioned that we both had our serious concerns about Larry—that he twice interrupted us and made us feel uncomfortable. She then confided that she too was uncomfortable with Larry working there at night and that there were other issues she didn't want to share regarding his character and "habits." She said she was probably going to soon let him go.

I wish I had a more colorful and dramatic way to end this story, but I don't. I think that's probably a good thing. Several months later Marc asked his Reiki instructor how his sister was and how things were going at Our Lady of Sorrows. He told Marc as far as he knew things were going fine. In this case, I'm hoping no news is good news.

|||||||||||||||||||||||||||||||||||||||||||||||||||||||||||||||||||||||||||||||||||||||||||||||||||||||||||||||||||||||||||||||||||||||||

IT'S ALL IN YOUR HEAD ...
YOU JUST HAVE NO IDEA
HOW BIG YOUR HEAD IS

... come now, grant me an easy life for my song.
And still again may I pray to sing you a song.

HOMER, HYMN TO DEMETER

It's Christmas morning 2009—as good a time as any to fin-
ish a book. So far in this incarnation I've seen sixty-two Christmas mornings. I'm sure they are all worthy to be enshrined in my
memory, but sadly, many are now unremembered or else lie buried deep beneath more recent and dramatic memories. Forgotten
or not, Christmas has always been very magical for me. I guess it
is for many people. Long after I rejected the Christian faith, I still
held fast to the sacredness of Christmas. For me it is the celebration
not of the stern and angry father-god, or the loving and nurturing
mother-goddess, but of the child-god, crowned and conquering. I

confess, even at my age, I feel like a child. That's got to be a good thing in an Aeon when God is a Child.

And so, I'm always extra restless on Christmas morning—restless, like a child who doesn't know which new toy to play with first. Restless to create something with my energy. One Christmas morning about thirty years ago, I got up early and melted a bagful of candle stubs into a round Christmas cookie tin. I munched cookies while I waited for the wax to cool in the refrigerator. Then I popped the thick wax disk out of the tin and set to work carving the intricate design of Dr. John Dee's famous Sigillium Dei Aemeth. Constance made me do this messy, waxy work out on the cold back porch, but I didn't care. It was my Christmas present to my child-self, and a very good present it has turned out to be. I immediately put it to work contacting angels and it has remained the centerpiece of my Enochian magical work these thirty-odd (very odd) years. Like a magick carpet, it has carried me around the world; it has been the inspiration for two books and countless classes, lectures, and workshops. Most importantly, it has helped me travel to other worlds, other dimensions—heavens.

Can I truthfully say (like the title of this chapter suggests) that all this magick, all these experiences have merely taken place "in my head"?

Yes. I am saying that. "It's all in your head." But please do not forget the second part of my outrageous statement, "you just have no idea how big your head is!" As I observed earlier, mind and consciousness transcend the boundaries of the brain, transcend the boundaries of time and space. That's how big my head is! Nothing can happen outside of it because there is no outside of it.

When I close my eyes, where are the sun and moon and planets and stars? Where are the Aethyrs and the Sephiroth, and the hierarchy of gods, archangels, angels, spirits and intelligences and demons? They are in my head—that's where they live. That's where they are real to me—and that's where they live, that's where they are real to me when I open my eyes also.

Am I suggesting that all of your magick—all of your experiences—all of your universe is merely taking place in your head?

I am tempted to say, "Yes!"

But, to be perfectly honest with you, I can't say for sure. Because, although I'm pretty sure I exist, I can never be absolutely sure about you.

||||||||||||||||||||||||||||||||||||||||||||||||||||||||||||||||||||||||||||||||||||||||||||||||||||||||||

MY BROTHER
REMEMBERS OUR FATHER

My life has always been filled with magical events and personalities. In chapter 4, I told how my father had an oddly mystical influence on my brother Marc and myself. In chapter 13, I mention my brother's psychic and healing abilities. For the reader who would like a little more insight on both these subjects, I offer this brief appendix. It is a chapter from my brother Marc's autobiography. This little story took place when I was two years old, and provides, I believe, a poignant window onto the character of these two precious magical beings in my life.

ONCE UPON A TIME

Excerpt from Orange Sunshine—
How I Almost Survived America's Cultural Revolution.[1]

Dad was not a religious man. Mom accused him of being an atheist. She once whispered to me, in a conspiratorial tone of voice, that Darwin's *Origin of Species* was his Bible. Naturally, I wanted to be an atheist and read Charles Darwin. I wanted to be just like my dad. Thus, I was very surprised by what he asked me to do.

I had just gotten home from school, and was in the kitchen looking for a snack. Dad was on his way to work. He paused on his way out the door, and squatted down eye-level to me. He smelled of cigarettes and appeared very somber.

"Son, the little boy who lives in back of us is real sick. His mom accidentally slammed his hand in the car door. The doctors fixed his hand but he hurt it again. He was playing in his yard and got dirt and dog poop under his bandages. The wound got infected, and he's back in the hospital. The doctors don't think he'll live. He's got lockjaw. Would you please pray for him, son? God listens to you."

Dad stood up, grabbed his black metal lunchbox, and without another word, went off to his job in the oil fields. I was eight years old and had no idea why my dad thought "God listens" to me. I didn't know what tetanus was. I visualized a little boy lying in a hospital bed with a huge lock around his jaw. I silently prayed, "God, if it be your will, please let the little neighbor boy live. Amen." I didn't

1 Marc DuQuette, *Orange Sunshine*, pp. 1–2.

know the kid. I thought my prayer was very half-assed and insincere.

Several days later, I overheard Mom and another neighbor talking about the little boy. They said he was making a full recovery and would be home soon. Dad never again spoke of his prayer request, so I haven't mentioned it until now.

||||||||||||||||||||||||||||||||||||||||||||||||||||||||||||||||||||||||||||||||||||||||||||||||||||||||||||||||||||||||||||

APOSTOLIC SUCCESSION

In chapters 6 and 13, I refer to my credentials as a bishop. I thought the reader would appreciate a little more information. Throughout the years, I have received at the hands of several individuals representing various denominational lines of succession consecration in no fewer than thirty apostolic lines of succession including: the Antiochian–Jacobite Succession; the Roman-Old Catholic Succession; Armenian Uniate; Syro-Chaldean; Anglican, Celtic Origin; American Greek Melchite; Orthodox Patriarchate; (Constantinople); Russian Orthodox; Non Juring Bishops of Scotland; Syrian-Malabar; Syrian-Gallican; Coptic; Coptic Uniate; Anglican, Non-Celtic; Irish; Welsh; Mariavite; Old Greek Melchite (Byzantine); Old Armenian; Corporate Reunion; Chaldean Uniate; Polish National Catholic—Albanian; Liberal Catholic; African Orthodox Catholic Church; Dutch Old Catholic (Utrecht); Gallican Catholic; Italian National Catholic; Vintrasian Carmelite; Byzantine Orthodox Catholic; Brazilian National Catholic; Haitian Independent; Old Catholic Orthodox.

For example, the details of just one line of succession, that of
The Roman-Old Catholic, list goes like this:

Saint Peter became Bishop of Rome in 38 AD; Peter consecrated (2) Linus in 67 AD; who in turn consecrated (3)
Ancletus [Cletus] in 76 who consecrated (4) Clement in
88 who consecrated (5) Evaristus in 97 then—(6) Alexander I, 105; (7) Sixtus I, 115; (8) Telesphorus, 125; (9)
Hygimus, 136; (10) Pius I, 140; (11) Anicetus, 155; (12)
Soter, 166; (13) Eleutherius, 175; (14) Victor I, 189; (15)
Zephyrinus, 199; (16) Callistus I, 217; (17) Urban I, 222;
(18) Pontian, 230; (19) Anterus, 235; (20) Fabian, 236;
(21) Cornelius, 251; (22) Lucius I, 253; (23) Stephen I,
254; (24) Sixtus II, 257; (25) Dionysius, 259; (26) Felix I,
269; (27) Eutychian, 275; (28) Caius, 283; (29) Marcel-
linus, 296; (30) Marcellus I, 308; (31) Eucebius, 309; (32)
Melchiades [Miltiades], 311; (33) Sylvester I, 314; (34)
Marcus, 336; (35) Julius I, 337; (36) Liberius, 352; (37)
Damasus I, 366; (38) Siricius, 384; (39) Anastasius I, 399;
(40) Innocent I, 401; (41) Zosimus, 417; (42) Boniface I,
418; (43) Celestine I, 422; (44) Sixtus III, 432; (45) Leo
I, 440; (46) Hilary, 461; (47) Simplicius, 468; (48) Felix
III, 483; (49) Gelasius I, 492; (50) Anastasius II, 496; (51)
Symmachus, 498; (52) Hormisdas, 514; (53) John I, 523;
(54) Felix IV, 526; (55) Boniface II, 530; (56) John II,
535; (57) Agapitus, 535; (58) Sylverius, 536; (59) Vigilus,
537; (60) Pelagius I, 556; (61) John III, 561; (62) Benedict I, 575; (63) Pelagius II, 579; (64) Gregory I, 590; (65)
Sabinianus, 604; (66) Boniface III, 607; (67) Boniface IV,
608; (68) Deusdedit [Adeodatus I], 615; (69) Boniface V,
619; (70) Honorius, 625; (71) Severinus, 640; (72) John
IV, 640; (73) Theodore I, 642; (74) Martin I, 649; (75)

Eugene I, 654; (76) Vitalian, 657; (77) Adeodatus II, 672; (78) Donus, 676; (79) Agatho, 678; (80) Leo II, 682; (81) Benedict II, 684; (82) John V, 685; (83) Conon, 686; (84) Sergius I, 687; (85) John VI, 701; (86) John VII, 705; (87) Sisinnius, 708; (88) Constantine, 708; (89) Gregory II, 715 (90) Gregory III, 731; (91) Zachary, 741; (92) Stephen II, 752; (93) Paul I, 757; (94) Stephen III, 768; (95) Adrian I, 772; (96) Leo III, 795; (97) Stephan IV, 816; (98) Paschal I, 817; (99) Eugene II, 824; (100) Valentine, 827; (101) Gregory IV, 827; (102) Sergius II, 844; (103) Leo IV, 847; (104) Benedict III, 855; (105) Nicholas I The Great, 858 (106) Adrian II, 867; (107) John VIII, 872; (108) Marinus I, 882; (109) Adrian III, 884; (110) Stephan V, 885; (111) Formosus, 891; (112) Boniface VI; (113) Steven VI, 897; (114) Romanus, 897; (115) Theodore II, 897; (116) John IX, 898; (117) Benedict IV, 900; (118) Leo V, 903; (119) Sergius III, 904; (120) Anastasius III, 911; (121) Landus, 913; (122) John X, 914; (123) Leo VI, 938; (124) Stephan VII, 928; (125) John XI, 931; (126) Leo VII, 936; (127) Stephen VIII, 939; (128) Maginus II, 942; (129) Agapitus II, 946; (130) John XIII, 955; (131) Leo VII, 963; (132) Benedict V, 964; (133) John XIV, 965; (134) Benedict VI, 973; (135) Benedict VII, 974; (136) John XIV, 983, (137) John XV, 985; (138) Gregory V, 996; (139) Sylvester II, 999; (140) John XVII, 1003; (141) John XVIII, 1004; (142) Sergius IV, 1009; (143) Benedict VIII, 1012; (144) John XIX, 1024; (145) Benedict IX, 1032; (146) Sylvester III, 1045; (147) Benedict IX [Second time], 1045; (148) Gregory VI, 1045; (149) Clement II, 1046; (150) Benedict IX [Third time], 1047; (151) Damasus II, 1048; (152) Leo IX, 1049; (153) Victor II, 1055; (154) Stephan IX, 1057; (155) Nicholas II, 1059; (156) Alexander II, 1061; (157)

Gregory VII, 1073; (158) Victor III, 1087; (159) Urban II, 1088; (160) Paschal II, 1099; (161) Gelasius II, 1118; (162) Callistus II, 1119; (163) Honorius II, 1124; (164) Innocent II, 1130; (165) Celestine II, 1143; (166) Lucius II, 1144; (167) Eugene III, 1145; (168) Anastasius IV, 1153; (169) Adrian IV, 1154; (170) Alexander III, 1159; (171) Lucius III, 1181; (172) Urban III, 1185; (173) Gregory VIII, 1187; (174) Clement III, 1187; (175) Celestine III, 1191; (176) Innocent III, 1198; (177) Honorius III, 1216; (178) Gregory IX, 1227; (179) Celestine IV, 1241; (180) Innocent IV, 1243; (181) Alexander IV, 1254; (182) Urban IV, 1261; (183) Clement IV, 1265; (184) Gregory X, 1271; (185) Innocent V, 1276; (186) Adrian V, 1276; (187) John XXI, 1276; (188) Nicholas III, 1277; (189) Martin IV, 1281; (190) Honorius IV, 1285; (191) Nicholas IV, 1288; (192) Celestine V, 1294; (193) Boniface VIII, 1294; (194) Benedict XI, 1303; (195) Clement V, 1305; (196) John XXII, 1316; (197) Benedict XII, 1334; (198) Clement VI, 1342; (199) Innocent VI, 1352; (200) Urban V, 1362; (201) Gregory XI, 1370; (202) Urban VI, 1378; (203) Boniface IX, 1389; (204) Innocent VII, 1389; (205) Gregory XII, 1406; (206) Martin V, 1417; (207) Eugene IV, 1431; (208) Nicholas V, 1447; (209) Callistus III, 1455; (210) Pius II, 1458; (211) Paul II, 1464; (212) Sixtus IV, 1471; (213) Innocent VIII, 1484; (214) Alexander VI, 1492; (215) Pius III, 1503; (216) Julius II, 1503; (217) Leo X, 1513; (218) Adrian VI, 1522; (219) Clement VII, 1523; (220) Paul III, 1534; (221) Julius III, 1550; (222) Marcellus II, 1555; (223) Paul IV, 1555; (224) Pius IV, 1559; (225) Pius V, 1566; (226) Gregory XIII, 1572; (227) Sixtus V, 1585; (228) Urban VII, 1590; (229) Gregory XIV, 1590; (230) Innocent IX, 1591; (231)

Clement VIII, 1592; (232) Leo XI, 1605; (233) Paul V, 1605; (234) Gregory, XV 1621; (235) Urban VIII, 1623; (236) Innocent X, 1644; (237) Alexander VII, 1655; (238); Antonio Barberini, 1655; (239) Michael le Tellier, 1668; (240) Jaques Benigne de Bousseut, 1670; (241) James Coyon de Matignon, 1693; (242) Dominicus Marie Varlet, 1719; (243) Cornelius Van Steenhoven, 1724; (244) Johannes Van Stiphout, 1745; (245) Gaultherus Michael Van Niewenhuizen, 1786; (246) Adrian Brockman, 1778; (247) Johannes Jacobus Van Rhijin, 1797; (248) Gilbertus de Jong, 1805; (249) Wilibrordus Van Os, 1814; (250) Johannes Bon, 1819; (251) Johannes Van Santen, 1825; (252) Hermanus Heijkamp, 1854; (253) Casparus Johannes Rinkel, 1873; (254) Geradus Gul, 1892. (255) Arnold Harris Matthew, 1908 (by Archbishop Gul of Utrecht, assisted by Bishop J. J. Van Thiel of Haarlem, Bishop N. B. P. Spit of Deventer, and Bishop J. Demmel of Bonn, Germany, to serve as the First Old Catholic Bishop of Britain. Continuation in the United States: (256) Fredrick Wiloughby, 1914; (257) James I. Wedgewood, 1916; (258) Irving S. Cooper, 1919; (259) Charles Hampton, 1931. Hampton was Principal consecrator of (260) Herman A. Spruit, consecrator of (261) Lewis S. Keizer; (262) Alberto LaCava (1995); (263) Emanuele Coltro exchanged consecrations with Alberto LaCava, 19 November 2000 in Yonkers, New York; (264) Phillip A. Garver, 16 February 2001 in Verona, Italy; (265) Lon Milo DuQuette, 10 March 2001 in Akron, Ohio, USA.

BIBLIOGRAPHY

Crowley, Aleister. *The Book of the Goetia of Solomon the King. Translated into the English Tongue by a Dead Hand and Adorned with Divers Other Matter Germane Delightful to the Wise, the Whole Edited, Verified, Introduced and Commented by Aleister Crowley.* Most recent edition with engraved illustrations of the spirits by M. L. Breton and foreword by Hymenaeus Beta (York Beach, ME: Samuel Weiser, 1996). Known as the *Lesser Key of Solomon*, it is the First Book of the Lemegeton (c. 1687). Translated by S. L. MacGregor Mathers (the "Dead Hand" referred to in the full title above). From the British Library Sloane Manuscripts nos. 2731 and 3648.

———. *Collected Works, Orpheus. Vol. III.* Homewood, IL: Yogi Publications, 1978.

———. *The Equinox I* (6). Fall 1911, ed. Soror Virakam, London. Reprinted York Beach, ME: Weiser Books, Inc., 1992.

———. *Liber Libræ Sub Figura XXX, The Book of the Balance*, and *Magick, Liber ABA, Book Four.* Second Revised Edition, ed. Hymenaeus Beta. York Beach, ME: Weiser Books, Inc., 1997. p. 668. *Liber Libræ* itself was taken from a Golden Dawn paper, "On the General Guidance and Purification of the Soul."

———. *The Qabalah of Aleister Crowley.* New York: Weiser Books, Inc., 1973. Retitled *777 and Other Qabalistic Writings of Aleister Crowley* in the fifth printing, 1977. Reprinted York Beach, ME: Weiser Books, Inc., 1990.

DuQuette, Lon Milo. *Accidental Christ: The Story of Jesus as Told by His Uncle.* Chicago: Thelesis Aura, 2006.

————. *Angels, Demons & Gods of the New Millennium.* York Beach, ME: Weiser Books, Inc., 1997.

————. *The Chicken Qabalah of Rabbi Lamed Ben Clifford.* York Beach, ME: Weiser Books, Inc., 2001.

————. *Enochian Vision Magick—An Introduction and Practical Guide to the Magick of Dr. John Dee and Edward Kelley.* York Beach, ME: Weiser Books, Inc., 2008.

————. *The Magick of Thelema.* York Beach, ME: Weiser Books, Inc., 1993.

————. *My Life with the Spirits: The Adventures of a Modern Magician.* York Beach ME: Weiser Books, Inc. 1999.

————. *Tarot of Ceremonial Magick.* York Beach, ME: Weiser Books, Inc., 1995.

DuQuette, Lon, and Constance DuQuette. *Tarot of Ceremonial Magick: A Pictorial Synthesis of Three Great Pillars of Magick (Astrology, Enochian Magick, Goetia).* Originally published by U.S. Games Systems, Inc., 1994. Newest edition by Thelesis Aura, 2010.

DuQuette, Marc E. *Orange Sunshine—How I Almost Survived America's Cultural Revolution.* (Los Angeles CA: Marc DuQuette, 2008).

Lamsa, George M. (trans.). *The Holy Bible from Ancient Eastern Manuscripts.* Translated from Aramaic. Philadelphia, PA: A.J. Holman Company, 1967.

Lévi, Eliphas. Pseudonym of Alphonse Louis Constant. *Dogme et ritual de la haute magie* was first published in 1854. Published most recently as *Transcendental Magic* translated by A.E. Waite. York Beach, ME: Weiser Books, Inc., 2001.

Regardie, Israel. *The Complete Golden Dawn System of Magic.* Third revised limited edition. Reno, NV: New Falcon Publications, 2008.

Wihelm, Richard, and Cary Baynes, translators. *The I Ching or Book of Changes.* New York: Bollingen Foundation Inc., 1950. Third edition reprinted with corrections, Princeton University Press, 1969.

INDEX